THE ILLUSTRATED
ATLAS OF
HAWAI'I

INCLUDING A BRIEF HISTORY OF HAWAI'I BY GAVAN DAWS

EDITED BY O.A. BUSHNELL

WRITTEN BY GAVAN DAWS, O.A. BUSHNELL,
AND ANDREW BERGER

INTERIOR ILLUSTRATIONS BY JOSEPH FEHER, MARTIN CHARLOT,
BJORNE SKRIMSTAD, AND ROGELIO SUGA

COVER ILLUSTRATION BY HERB KAWAINUI KANE

Published and distributed by

ISLAND HERITAGE™
P U B L I S H I N G
A DIVISION OF THE MADDEN CORPORATION

94-411 KŌʻAKI STREET, WAIPAHU, HAWAIʻI 96797-2806
ORDERS: (800) 468-2800
INFORMATION: (808) 564-8800
FAX: (808) 564-8877
islandheritage.com

Library of Congress Catalog Number 74-152566
ISBN# : 1-59700-839-7
First Edition, First Printing - 2009

INTRODUCTION

Herald with Conch

The Pacific Ocean is enormous—more than 10,000 miles north to south, more than 10,000 miles east to west at its widest. In area it is more than 70,000,000 square miles, by far the biggest single feature of the globe.

Polynesia, of which the Hawaiian Islands form a part, occupies an area roughly triangular in shape. South of the equator, the extremities of the triangle are New Zealand in the west and Easter Island in the east. Hawai'i is the third extremity, north of the equator in the vicinity of the Tropic of Cancer.

This location, more than 2,000 miles from the nearest point of the American continent, more than 2,000 miles from the nearest major island group to the south, makes the Hawaiian Islands the most isolated archipelago in the world. This, together with the fact that the total land area of the Hawaiian chain is less than 6,500 square miles, makes it understandable that discovery and settlement by a native population did not take place until late in the world's history—on recent evidence, perhaps as late as the third century A.D.

Westerners came upon Hawai'i for the first time something like fifteen hundred years later—in the eighteenth century. It was immediately obvious to the white men that the Hawaiians were physically and culturally related to islanders in other parts of the Polynesian triangle south of the equator. Equally clearly Polynesians as a whole were different from the other broadly recognizable groups of islanders in the Pacific, Melanesians, and Micronesians.

Considering the vastness of the Pacific, and the enormous difficulty experienced by white men in sailing it and plotting the positions of the principal islands—a process that took them more than 250 years—the achievement of the Polynesians in locating and peopling their islands could only be described as remarkable. Their origins and their migrations among the islands of the great triangle were always matters for speculation. In 1976 traditional ocean voyaging was revived, proving that Hawaiians had used ancient southern sea routes to settle the islands of Hawai'i.

The Polynesians themselves had an elaborate tradition of their origins and history, maintained in religious, genealogical, and narrative chants. During the nineteenth and twentieth centuries, a good many traditions were set down in writing by interested white men and by natives with a Western education. And, scholarly studies have been made, reconciling the traditions of one island group with those of another and trying to connect the traditions of Polynesia as a whole.

Often it was possible for scholars to put together a likely sequence of historical events, but to assign a reliable Western chronology was difficult because the Polynesians dated events no more exactly than by generations or the reigns of chiefs. Accordingly, if, for example, a generation was taken by a scholar to be 25 years on the average, rather than 30, an event mentioned as taking place 20 generations in the Polynesian past could be located only in a given century, not in a particular year or even a particular decade.

This kind of difficulty reappears in studies of the Polynesian language itself. It is possible to make an extensive list of words common to all of Polynesia, and to note how in different island groups a word retains its meaning but changes its pronunciation. With a sufficiently large body of evidence, it would be possible to make hypotheses about the length of time the population of one island group had been separated from another, giving these changes time to develop. And from this, other hypotheses might be made about the direction of migration. But again, this useful linguistic work does not yield precise results in historical terms.

Physical anthropologists have studied the skeletal remains of ancient Polynesians and have compared them with the physiques of modern-day Polynesians, in the hope of determining relationships within Polynesia, and with other parts of the Pacific. Parallel studies have been made in serology to determine the occurrence of different blood types among modern islanders, again in an effort to learn something of their origins, dispersal, and eventual groupings. Again, the results have been useful but inconclusive.

The science most likely to solve the Polynesian puzzle—if indeed a solution is possible—is archaeology: the systematic study of plant, animal, and settlement remains recoverable in historical sequence above and below ground in the islands. Archaeological work of permanent usefulness is relatively recent in Polynesia—its beginnings only a century in the past—and a great deal more work is needed. But already, the outlines of the migrations that settled Hawai'i from south of the equator are much clearer than they have ever been, and the larger question of the general origins of the Polynesians is being answered more and more.

Hawaiians believed that words bind, and words make free. While mortals looked on in awe, sacred chants and worshipful dances were offered to the gods.

CONTENTS

POLYNESIA ORIGINS AND MIGRATIONS

The first Hawaiians came from south of the equator, from the Marquesas Islands and the Society Islands of central Polynesia. But where did the central Polynesians come from in turn? Archeological findings, together with studies of winds, currents, flora, and fauna, suggest that the origin of the Polynesian culture was in the western Pacific.

Linguistic studies support this idea. The vocabulary of the Polynesian islanders is related to a widely dispersed language family extending west across Southeast Asia—as far west, indeed, as Madagascar.

Current theory suggests that the major island complex of Samoa-Tonga is the first place where a distinct Polynesian culture developed. A characteristic physical type and social organization were then spread by migration to develop in specialized ways on widely separated island groups. The Society Islands and neighboring archipelagoes were evidently stepping-off places for migratory voyages to the extremities of Polynesia: Easter Island, New Zealand, and Hawai'i.

In opposition to this general body of theory and evidence is the work of Thor Heyerdahl. He devoted a great part of his active life to the idea that the origin of Polynesian culture is not Asian but American. Certain elements of the Polynesia flora and fauna are American in origin, and Heyerdahl's own Kon-Tiki raft expedition demonstrated that human contact was possible between the Pacific coast of South America and Polynesia. However, the 1976 revival of traditional Polynesian voyaging in Hawai'i essentially disproved his theories of origin. The weight of available evidence, as indicated, favors an Asian origin.

As far as the narrower question of the immediate origin of Hawaiian culture is concerned, archeological findings, including dating of material by radio-carbon techniques, have now made it possible to say with some certainty that the first permanent settlements were made by migrants from the Marquesas Islands in about the third century A.D. Also, subsequent migrations from the Society Islands

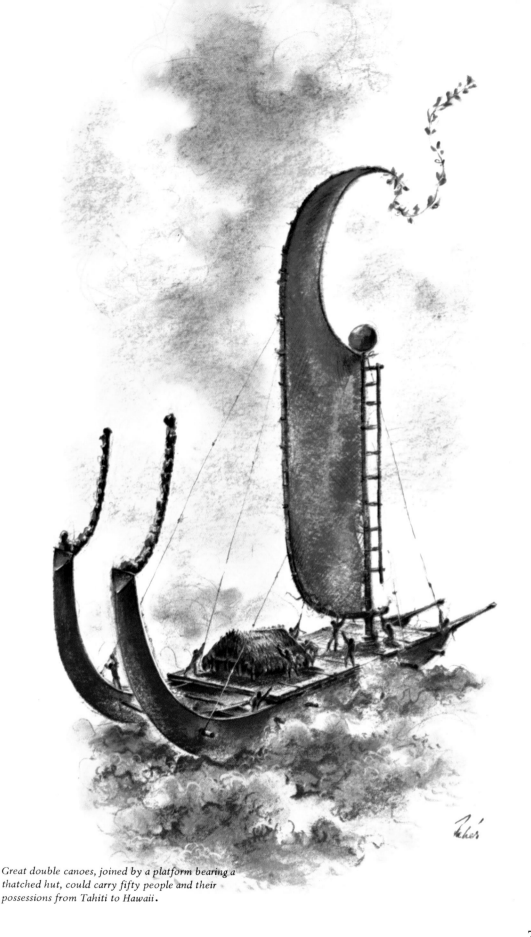

Great double canoes, joined by a platform bearing a thatched hut, could carry fifty people and their possessions from Tahiti to Hawaii.

between the eleventh and fourteenth centuries A.D. established the culture which, in a developed form, was brought to Western eyes by the discoveries of white explorers in the late eighteenth century.

Quite apart from the question of origins, the navigational techniques of the Polynesians have fascinated Westerners. Hawaiian traditions, for example, speak of two-way voyages between Hawai'i and Tahiti, a distance of more than 2,000 miles of open-ocean. What clouds the question is that at the time of the Western discoveries, such voyages had ceased, taking the old technical knowledge and, perhaps the old confidence, which led to an apparent loss of such methods. White men have tried endlessly to reconstruct, on paper and in practice, the techniques which enabled the Polynesians, without sailing ships of large size and deep draught and quite without Western instruments and maps, to find for the first time, and then find again, island groups so widely separated.

The big double-hulled, decked and roofed oceanic sailing canoes, in which the migratory voyages must have been made, were still being used for shorter inter-island voyages when the white discoverers came to Polynesia, and detailed drawings of them by Westerners survived. In 1976 a scientific expedition called the Hōkule'a, using a 60-foot canoe built according to ancient Polynesian design and sailed by traditional Polynesian navigational techniques, journeyed from Hawai'i to Tahiti and back, demonstrating the feasibility of such voyages. On a more theoretical level, computer studies have been made to work out the probabilities of success and failure in oceanic voyaging in Polynesia over a long period of time.

One outdated theory was that Polynesia could have been peopled by random one-way voyages—that is to say, more or less accidentally, by castaways, political exiles, and adventurers.

Evidence suggests that seafarers from the Marquesas settled near South Point, Hawaii. Unless they arrived fully equipped, they would have had to make at least one voyage home for food plants and animals.

Given enough time, and enough canoes swept into unknown waters by changing winds and currents, survivors would have found new archipelagoes and settled them. This theory, of course, does not really account for the existing traditional evidence of two-way voyaging between an island homeland and a newly-settled archipelago a great distance away. Apart from anything else, two-way voyaging argues a considerable knowledge of astronomy, which obviously would have to be built up over a period of time. Current reconstructions suggest that the Polynesians' astronomical knowledge was excellent, and that they were extremely skilled sea-goers—as would be expected from their adaptation to life on small islands in a great ocean.

ANCIENT HAWAIIAN SOCIETY

Estimates of the Hawaiian population in the late eighteenth century, the time of the Western discovery, range from as low as about 150,000 to as high as about 400,000. Contemporary research suggests between 250,000 and 1 million. By then the Hawaiians were well settled on the major islands of the chain—Hawaiʻi itself, the biggest island, Maui, Molokaʻi, Lānaʻi, Kahoʻolawe, Oʻahu, Kauaʻi, and Niʻihau.

The characteristic terrain of the islands—rugged inland mountains, with valleys more or less suitable for agriculture leading out to narrow coastal flatlands and coral reefs in the shallow water—encouraged this settlement pattern of small dispersed groups, and probably did something in turn to encourage a political development along tribal rather than unitary lines.

The typical landholding pattern was based on a unit called the *ahupuaʻa*, ideally a wedge-shaped area of land extending from the mountains to the sea, within which all the necessities of life could be found. The basic occupations were agriculture and fishing. The two staple items of the Hawaiian diet were fish and *poi*, a paste made from the cooked and pounded root of taro, grown in the valleys in ingenious and carefully tended irrigated plantations. This diet was supplemented by the meat of pigs, chickens, and dogs, and various fruits, including the coconut

Warriors from Tahiti conquered the pioneer menehune. *Taller, stronger, haughtier, and claiming the great gods as ancestors, these were the* aliʻi, *the new rulers of Hawaiʻi.*

and the banana.

The Hawaiian religion bore a general resemblance to that of other Polynesian island groups. Four principle gods, all male—Kū, Kāne, Lono and Kanaloa—exercised ultimate jurisdiction over human activity, and countless minor gods and spirit beings were present as forces in the natural world. The gods had created the world and all that was in it. Men going about their daily occupations were constantly aware of this. The calendar of the month and the year was based on ritual observances. The most powerful human beings among the Hawaiians were the high chiefs, the *ali'i*, and their priests, who were most closely in touch with the gods. The most imposing structure erected by the Hawaiians was the stone-platformed *heiau*, or religious temple.

The organizing principle of Hawaiian religion, and of Hawaiian society generally, was that of *kapū*, or taboo. There were *kapū* people, places, things, and times. They were sacred, and any profanation of their sacredness was held to be extremely dangerous and disturbing to the well-being of individuals and the equilibrium of society. Thus, a tremendously involved and detailed code of behavior grew up, regulating the relationships of the individual Hawaiian with his contemporaries, with his ancestors and descendants, and with his natural surroundings, with the world at large.

At the time of the Western discovery, no single chief had control of the whole island chain. Rather, on each island, one or more chiefs of high birth, political talent and military ambition were contestants for power.

War among the competing chiefs was a constant possibility and a frequent actuality. But total war was not feasible. The economy of the islands was basically a subsistence economy and could not stand long periods of wasteful unproductiveness. By the eighteenth century, evidently, the population had grown to a point where the resources of the islands were beginning to be strained, and extensive destruction and prolonged neglect of agriculture would not have been supportable. Thus, although the ambition of the chiefs was comprehensive, war in practice was confined to sporadic raiding of enemy territory by bands of warriors rather than massed invasions by all able-bodied men.

As long as there was no single conquering chief, the power of all Hawaiian *ali'i* was limited to some degree. Whether, undisturbed by contact with the West, Hawaiian society could have maintained its complex governing system is problematical. Certainly the chances for new experiments in power politics provided by the appearance of white men with an advanced military technology transformed Hawaiian traditional society in the space of one or two generations.

The Hawaiian Islands were the last in Polynesia, and the last major group in the Pacific, to come under the notice of Westerners. This can be explained, once again, by their isolated location in the north central Pacific. Throughout the age of Pacific exploration, from the early sixteenth to the late eighteenth century, Europeans on voyages of discovery characteristically entered the Pacific Ocean in the south, either by rounding the extremities of South America in the east, or by rounding the Cape of Good Hope at the foot of Africa in the west and crossing the Indian Ocean to enter the western Pacific. In either case, the wind and current systems of the southern hemisphere repeatedly made voyages exhaustingly long, thus reducing the opportunities for systematic canvases of the northern ocean.

Hawai'i eluded Europe's mariners for 268 years after they entered the Pacific. In 1624-1625 eleven Dutch ships, the "Nassau Fleet," sailed from America to Guam at latitudes too far south to discover Hawai'i.

The history of exploration in the Pacific reflects the changing imperial fortunes of the European powers. Broadly, the sixteenth century belonged to Spain. The first trans-Pacific voyage, that of Ferdinand Magellan in 1519, was part also of the first circumnavigation of the earth, and it was carried out under the auspices of the Spanish court. Later Spanish settlements in South and Central America laid a base for voyages between Mexico and Spain's colony in the Philippines.

The presence of Spain's Manila galleons in the northern Pacific for two centuries has led to speculation that the Spanish must surely, at one time or another, deliberately or inadvertently, have located the Hawaiian Islands. There is fragmentary evidence in Hawaiian tradition of the landing of a party of white men at some undetermined time, and attempts have been made by scholars to link this with Spanish records of shipwreck or expeditions off course. Hawai'i would certainly have been a useful discovery for the Spanish. For all this, the historical records of Spain remain silent on the subject. The known track of the Manila galleons took them south of Hawai'i on the way from Mexico to the Philippines and far to the north on the return voyage. Speculation on the subject remains no more than speculation.

As the sixteenth century was Spain's, so in general the seventeenth century in Pacific exploration belonged to the Netherlands. In strict terms, they were interlopers in the overseas domains marked out for Portugal and Spain, but Dutchmen on the far side of the earth could not be expected to trouble themselves much on such scores. Their contributions to geographical knowledge came as a by-product of their commercial ventures. Characteristically, they entered the Pacific from the west and confined themselves for the most part to the western Pacific. Even the voyages of their greatest navigator, Abel Tasman, did not approach Hawai'i.

The Spanish were interested in the legendary riches of undiscovered places and in the salvation of souls among the heathen natives they encountered. The Dutch were more prosaic men of commerce. The eighteenth century brought Frenchmen and Englishmen into the Pacific on voyages of discovery, and here the older motives for exploration were enriched by a genuine and powerful scientific and intellectual curiosity.

The major object of this curiosity was the mythical Great South Continent, whose existence had been postulated since classical times by geographers arguing that the land masses of the earth must have a certain symmetry about them, the south matching and balancing the north. At the opening of the modern age of exploration, as far as precise geographical knowledge was concerned, the Southern Continent might well have occupied any part of the southern Indian Ocean or the southern Pacific Ocean. Successive voyages

Captain James Cook, R.N. (1728-1779)

by French and English expeditions narrowed down its possible extent. But the tremendous difficulties involved in lengthy Pacific voyages—food shortages, disease, uncertainties about navigational position—left the Continent still a philosophical possibility, if an actual mystery, until the definitive voyages of James Cook.

And as far as the discovery of Hawai'i was concerned, continued concentration on the southern Pacific pushed the waters north of the equator into the second place. The existence of a major group of islands strategically located there, potentially very valuable to sea-going powers, remained unsuspected.

CAPTAIN COOK'S DISCOVERY

James Cook's first two voyages took him to the South Pacific. He entered the ocean for the first time in January 1769, en route to Tahiti to make astronomical observations of the transit of Venus across the face of the sun. In his secret instructions were provisions for the annexation of the Southern Continent, should he discover it. He did not, and neither did he on his second voyage, 1772-1775, during which he covered between 60,000 to 70,000 miles in southern waters.

If Cook could not find the much-discussed Southern Continent, it did not exist. He was the explorer's explorer—navigator, chart-maker, commander of ships, leader of men without peer, one of the greatest Englishmen of his day. His work gave detailed shape to Western understanding of the South Pacific, and he left only the most minor discoveries to be made there by his successors.

Two superbly successful voyages such as these encouraged the British government to send Cook on a third, this time to the North Pacific in search of another geographic will-of-the-wisp which had attracted the interest and attention of the European powers for centuries. Cook was to try to find a sea passage from the Pacific to the Atlantic, across the north of the American continent.

His track from the Society Islands to the west coast of North America led him to encounter the Hawaiian Islands. On the morning of January 18, 1778, Cook, with his two ships, HMS *Resolution* and HMS *Discovery*, raised the three western-most inhabited islands of the chain: O'ahu, Kaua'i, and Ni'ihau.

Cook went ashore at Waimea on Kaua'i and on Ni'ihau, spending two weeks in provisioning his ships and making a brief study of the Hawaiian people, their land, and their institutions.

Cook named his new discovery the Sandwich Islands, after the First Lord of the Admiralty. On February 2, he left for the American west coast and spent the better part of 1778 looking in vain for the sea passage. Turning south again to spend the winter in warmer latitudes before making another attempt at the discovery, he brought his ships to the eastern end of the Hawaiian chain, raising the island of Maui on November 25-26, 1778, and the island of Hawai'i immediately afterwards. He spent the last weeks of 1778 and the first of 1779 coasting Hawai'i. Not until he rounded the island's south point and set off along its west coast did he find what he was looking for: safe anchorage in a well-populated, well-supplied district. On January 17, he put in at Kealakekua Bay with the idea of remaining there for as long as it took to get his ships and men back in good condition for the arduous northern exploratory work that still lay ahead of them.

Cook had come at an important time in the Hawaiian religious year. Both his landfalls, first at Kaua'i in January 1778, then at Kealakekua in January 1779, took place during a festival known as the *makahiki*. For the Hawaiians, the god Lono was the deity of agricultural fertility, and it was believed that he made annual visits to his people around the turn of the year. To

In 1778, iron was so precious to Hawaiians that they offered a large hog in exchange for one English nail.

Honolulu was not an important location in ancient times. In 1816 it was a village of about 300 grass huts. Its population varied with the number of foreign ships anchored in the tiny harbor of Kou.

receive him, and to do him honor, the Hawaiians suspended work and war for several months at a time and spent their days in games and feasting, while the image of Lono was carried around the islands and the chiefs and priests collected goods in tribute under Lono's auspices.

In a sense this was highly fortunate for Cook. Many Hawaiians, tremendously impressed by the size of his ships and the strangeness of the men and equipment they carried, took Cook to be Lono himself. They heaped honors upon him and gifts of supplies upon the expedition.

On February 4, Cook left Kealakekua Bay, intending to look at some of the islands between Hawai'i and Kaua'i before going north again a second time. But a storm damaged the foremast of his flagship, HMS *Resolution*, and forced him to turn back to Kealakekua. Arriving there he found the rejoicing crowds of his earlier visit gone. The *makahiki* was over.

Cook's carpenters took the damaged foremast ashore, expecting repairs to take some days. On the night of February 13, some natives stole a ship's boat from the *Discovery*—a serious theft, and one which Cook could not disregard. He went ashore the next morning with a small party of marines, intending to bring the ruler of the island, the chief Kalani'ōpu'u, back to the *Resolution* as a hostage for the return of the boat. As the party was making its way down to the beach, a crowd of natives gathered. The mood of some of Kalani'ōpu'u's warriors turned ugly. There was a scuffle, which turned into a fight. Cook's men fired their guns. The Hawaiians attacked, and Cook was struck down and killed at the water's edge.

KAMEHAMEHA THE GREAT

The rise to power of the high chief Kamehameha, who became the first king of the Hawaiian Islands, coincided exactly with the opening of the era of contact with the West. Kamehameha was born in the Kohala district of the island of Hawai'i, probably about 1758, though the precise date is unknown. The ruler of the island of Hawai'i at that time was Kamehameha's uncle Kalaniōpu'u, who also controlled the Hāna district of eastern Maui. Arranging for the succession in anticipation of his death, he gave his son Kīwalaō charge of his lands, and to Kamehameha he gave charge of the highly important god Kūka'ilimoku, who was worshipped to bring success to the battlefield.

Argument and fighting took place over the distribution of land on Hawai'i, and it was Kamehameha's success in these local disputes that led him down a path of war, which brought him to control of almost the whole island group by 1795.

The great obstacle facing Kamehameha on the islands west of Hawai'i was the chief Kahekili, who controlled most of Maui and its neighboring islands, Moloka'i and Lāna'i, and had kinship ties with the rulers of O'ahu and Kaua'i. Kamehameha defeated Kahekili's son, Kalanikūpule, at the battle of 'Īao Valley on Maui, but not until after the death of Kahekili in 1794 did Kamehameha invade the island of O'ahu. A decisive campaign was fought there in 1795, when Kamehameha led a fleet of canoes and small Western schooners to the southern shores of O'ahu, landed, and pressed inland to the valley of Nu'uanu, where his men engaged and routed the forces of the heir of Kahekili, Kalanikūpule.

With victory at Nu'uanu, Kamehameha controlled all the major islands except Kaua'i and Ni'ihau. He made two attempts to invade Kaua'i over the years. In 1796 he set out with his fleet of canoes into the Kaua'i channel but had to turn back because of rough weather and high waves. And the more substantial fleet he assembled in 1804 to carry his men the length

Kamehameha I (1758?-1819)

15

of the chain from Hawai'i to Kaua'i had brought his army only as far as O'ahu when an epidemic (a Western disease, probably cholera) struck and decimated his army and the population of the island in general. Eventually, Kamehameha got what he wanted without fighting. In 1810 he reached an agreement with the ruling chief of Kaua'i that gave him suzerainty over Kaua'i and Ni'ihau.

Kamehameha's governmental organization was unique in the Pacific. No native chief of his day or later managed so completely to impose his will on an entire island chain—and, for that matter, on the white men who appeared in increasing numbers. To keep the control of the

Kamehameha II (1797-1824)

islands in his hands, Kamehameha appointed governors who reported directly to him—these men were chosen for their loyalty to him and also for their freedom from kinship ties with the old ruling chiefs. Kamehameha also made it a point of the greatest importance to build up a supply of Western arms, at the same time denying other chiefs the opportunity to collect guns. The other part of his arrangements, which ensured him continued dominance, was a constantly enforced, royal monopoly of trade. No chief or commoner was allowed to barter with Western ships on his own account. No Western captain, arriving with his ship, was allowed to begin trade anywhere in the islands

without Kamehameha's permission.

Cook's expedition did not traffic in arms with the Hawaiian chiefs, and the next Western ship to call at the islands did not appear until 1785. But every year after that, ships called with increasing frequency. Hawai'i became a way-station in a new sea-borne trade linking the northwest coast of America with China. The share of the islands in this trade was simple: the chiefs provided Western ships wintering in Hawai'i with food and supplies, and in return they asked for Western goods, with a great emphasis on iron and guns.

The same trade that brought Kamehameha his guns brought a great change in the settlement patterns of the islands. Honolulu harbor was discovered by Westerners, probably in 1794, though again the precise date is unknown. It was the only deep-water harbor in the islands, and with the Western ships putting in there as a matter of course, Honolulu became important enough for Kamehameha to move his court there in 1804.

BREAKING OF KAPŪ

Until about 1810, foreign trade remained much the same, with merchant ships calling at the islands for food and supplies. But then a new element appeared: Westerners discovered that the Hawaiian Islands had big stands of sandalwood trees. The aromatic wood was much in demand in China, and accordingly the new trade was added to the old. Again, Kamehameha kept a monopoly and used some of the proceeds to add to his always-growing collection of foreign ships. The sandalwood trade survived into the 1820s, declining sharply toward the end of that decade with the exhaustion of the sandalwood stands.

After his sojourn at Honolulu (1804-1812), Kamehameha decided to move back to his home island of Hawai'i. He had no more need for military campaigning, particularly after his agreement with the ruling chief of Kaua'i in 1810. And even though Honolulu was rapidly becoming the center of commerce, the king could rely on his governors to supervise trade efficiently.

By this time, Kamehameha was an elderly man. He lived out his last years on Hawai'i and died at something like seventy years of age in Kailua on May 8, 1819.

The question of the succession had been settled some years earlier, when Kamehameha named his son Liholiho as his heir. Another question, which could not be settled until the death of Kamehameha made it urgent, was whether the new form of government would survive the disappearance of the unifier.

Kamehameha had been a military conqueror and a political innovator, but he was always a conservative in matters of religion. In particular, he resisted any suggestion from white men that he might give up the old worship in favor of Christianity.

system discriminated against women in matters of behavior and even in matters of the foods that might safely be eaten, it is perhaps not surprising that when an attack on the *kapū* came, it originated among the female chiefs.

Kamehameha, in the course of his life, had had as many as twenty-one wives. Some of them survived him. The two most important and influential after his death were his favorite wife, Kaʻahumanu, and the mother of his two sons, Keōpūolani. In the months that followed Kamehameha's death, these two began to urge the new king, Liholiho, to flout the *kapū*.

The episode that followed is one of the strangest in the history of the Pacific, or indeed

of Kamehameha, inherited by Liholiho, were sufficient to stamp out the revolt, and Liholiho remained king.

Ruling as Kamehameha II (1819-1824), Liholiho never really settled down to the task of being a king. To follow such a formidable figure as his father would have been difficult in any circumstances. To lead a people who had just seen the *kapū* system dismantled was more difficult still. Liholiho, no more than a youth when he became king, found himself unable to control chiefs and commoners as Kamehameha the Great had done in maturity and old age. Restless and indecisive, the new king made only one important decision—to visit Great Britain

When the kapū *were abandoned, the gods lost their power.*

The position of the old religion, however, was no longer secure. In particular, the idea of *kapū* had come into question. In a way, the continuance of the *kapū* system depended on the continued isolation of the islands. Now that isolation was gone, the Hawaiians encountered for the first time a race of people, the Europeans, who could apparently break the *kapū* without punishment by the gods.

Evidently, in the forty years between Cook's visit and the death of Kamehameha, considerable skepticism about the *kapū* grew up among some Hawaiians, including several of the chiefs. In view of the fact that the *kapū*

of the world—a people giving up a religion system that had been theirs for centuries and not replacing it.

The events were simple but momentous. Kaʻahumanu and Keōpūolani eventually persuaded Liholiho to have a public feast at which women would be permitted to eat with men, and at which foods formerly forbidden to women would be served. This would symbolize the breaking of the *kapū*. The feast was served, the foods were eaten, the *kapū* were broken.

Some conservative chiefs on the island of Hawaiʻi took up arms in November 1819 in defense of the old system, but the armaments

and perhaps learn something of the art of ruling at the greatest royal court of the day. This was an uncertain venture, to say the least, and it turned out to be fatal. The Hawaiian royal party succumbed to disease in London, and Liholiho and his wife died there, of measles, in July 1824.

MERCHANTS AND MISSIONARIES

Two events during Liholiho's reign set the course of major developments during the reign of his successor, his younger brother, Kauikeaouli, the last son of Kamehameha the Great, who reigned as Kamehameha III (1825-1854). First, in the fall of 1819, American ships caught a whale off the coast of Hawai'i. Second, in the spring of the following year, 1820, American Protestant missionaries arrived in the Hawaiian kingdom. The whaling industry of the northern Pacific, dominated for the next fifty years by firms based in the New England port towns, turned Honolulu on O'ahu and Lahaina on Maui into the busiest ports in the Pacific, and tied the economic growth of Hawai'i to the United States. The missionary effort in turn was dominated by New Englanders and was just as important in linking the Hawaiian kingdom with the United States—perhaps more so.

After a great popular religious awakening among the commoners in the late 1820s, as many as 30 percent of the population could be claimed as members of the church by 1853. Without much doubt, the most important white men in the islands during the reign of Kamehameha III were Hiram Bingham, leader of the first missionaries to arrive in 1820; William Richards, who left the mission in the late 1830s to teach the chiefs the rudiments of Western government; and Gerrit Judd, a former missionary doctor, who became the chief minister of the government in the 1840s and early 1850s. For such men, inevitably, the idea of useful change among the Hawaiians was to make all the Kingdom's institutions, religious, educational, political, economic, as American as possible.

Beginning in 1838, the ruling chiefs of Kamehameha III began to take instruction in "political economy" from William Richards. In 1839 a declaration of rights was formulated, and in 1840 the first written constitution of the kingdom was framed and promulgated, establishing an elementary representative legislature (which included commoners among its members), setting out the government's executive powers, and inaugurating a supreme court.

Organic laws enacted in the middle 1840s made possible the further development of governmental machinery. A revision of the constituion in 1852 showed further American influence in the broadening of the franchise to something resembling universal male suffrage, balanced, however, by the continued existence of an upper house of hereditary high chiefs and royally appointed "nobles."

Beginning in the middle 1840s, a land commission supervised a series of arrangements known as the Great Mahele, or the great division, reapportioning land among crown, government, chiefs, and commoners, bringing in for the first time the Western principle of private ownership in land. By 1850 it was possible for a foreigner to purchase land in fee simple.

In all this, as remarked, American influence was strong. Great Britian and France were also interested in the islands of the Pacific, to the point of carrying out annexation in island groups in southern Polynesia. In the reign of Kamehameha III, Hawai'i faced threats to its independence from these two powers. More than once, French warships menaced Honolulu, their commanders insisting on the rights of French subjects there (including Catholic missionaries who arrived in 1827 but were

American missionaries

business men of Honolulu had had enough. In their view, Kalākaua's regime was ill-advised and corrupt. They, as heavy taxpayers, were being forced to finance the ruin of the islands. Led by Lorrin A. Thurston, an attorney and newspaper publisher descended from one of the first Protestant missionaries, they formed a political and military organization called the Hawaiian League, with the purpose of loosening Spreckels' grip on the economy, dislodging Gibson from the cabinet, and curbing the power of the king by a new constitution. By June 1887, they were ready for armed revolution.

The League was able to get what it wanted without bloodshed. After a mass meeting on June 30, 1887, and a show of arms, the king was presented with a set of demands, which had been drawn up and to which he agreed.

The "Bayonet Constitution" of 1887 limited the king's powers very severely and imposed a narrow franchise based on property, thus excluding perhaps three out of every four native Hawaiians from the vote. In 1887 as well, the reciprocity treaty was renewed; this time with the provision that the United States was to have the exclusive rights to develop and use Pearl Harbor as a naval station.

Unrest grew among the natives, and in July 1889, an attempt was made to overthrow the Bayonet Constitution. A part-Hawaiian named Robert Wilcox, who, as a youth, had been given a military and technical education abroad at royal expense, led a night raid on 'Iolani Palace at Honolulu on July 30, 1889 and occupied the building with 150 men, until gunfire forced his surrender after several hours.

Most Hawaiians considered Wilcox and his followers to be patriots. It was not clear whether he had acted with Kalākaua's consent. The king, for whatever reason, was not at the palace when Wilcox's party occupied it. Clearly, though, Wilcox was against the white revolutionaries of 1887, the men who now controlled the government. He was tried for treason, but native jurors acquitted him.

In 1890 economic difficulties returned. The United States changed its tariff policy, doing away with duties on imported sugar and replacing them with a bounty on sugar home-grown on the American mainland. This removed altogether Hawai'i's advantage under

Native supporters of the monarchy rose in two ineffective rebellions against the powerful businessmen who controlled the islands.

the reciprocity treaty. Sugar from the islands no longer had a protected market, and the Hawaiian industry entered into a deep depression.

This, together with a continued feeling that under a native monarchy white men in the islands would not have a government in their favor, led to a strong annexationist movement among Americans in Hawai'i.

Kalākaua died on January 20, 1891 in San Francisco during a visit to the west coast. He was succeeded by his sister Lili'uokalani (1891-1893). She was the last monarch of the Hawaiian kingdom. Her ideas of royal government were stronger even than those of Kalākaua, and there was no way that they could be reconciled with the articles of the constitution of 1887.

The two years of Lili'uokalani's reign were filled with heated political argument and complicated political maneuvers. In 1892 a secret Annexationist League was formed in Honolulu, and its membership based principally on that of the Hawaiian League of 1887 and including most notably Lorrin A. Thurston and another descendant of Protestant missionaries, Sanford B. Dole.

The queen and her foreign population, led by the Americans, were clearly heading for a collision. Lili'uokalani was determined to put power back into the hands of the ruling monarch; the Americans of the islands were equally determined to see that this never happened.

ANNEXATION

The collision came on January 14, 1893, when Lili'uokalani dissolved the legislature in session and let it be known that she was about to proclaim a new constitution. This led the annexationists to open revolution. They took to the streets of Honolulu with arms, and by January 17 were in control of principal government buildings. Very few shots were fired; no lives were lost. Lili'uokalani surrendered her powers, and a provisional government was proclaimed. The Hawaiian monarchy was at an end.

Sanford Dole, Lorrin Thurston, and the other revolutionary leaders hoped that the life of their provisional government would be short. They wanted nothing more than to see Hawai'i become American soil by annexation.

One immediate problem among several was that the United States Minister to Hawai'i, John L. Stevens, had been perhaps too quick to recognize the new regime. Indeed there was a case for saying that the presence of American troops, landed at Stevens' command from a warship in the harbor, had been a crucial factor in the success of the revolution. At least this was the view taken by the incoming Democratic administration of Grover Cleveland at Washington. After inquiries, an attempt was made by Cleveland to arrange for Lili'uokalani's reinstatement.

This ran aground on the determination of the revolutionaries, who on July 4, 1894,

Sanford Ballard Dole (1844-1926)

brought into effect a republican constitution and set about to wait until times were more favorable in Washington.

Lili'uokalani's supporters, mostly native, could not wait upon events. In January 1895, a counter-revolution, led once again by Robert Wilcox, put Honolulu and its surrounding valleys under arms for a few days. It was a lost cause. The royalists were easily put to flight, then systematically flushed out of their refuges. Once again, a series of treason trials was held, and Queen Lili'uokalani was given a sentence of house imprisonment.

During the entire life of the Hawaiian Republic, the question of annexation was debated at Washington. The United States had always been a continental nation. The acquisition of territories in distant places was a momentous step, not to be taken lightly. Still, expansionism was in the air in the 1890s. The doctrine that it was the nation's Manifest Destiny to become an imperial power was popular, especially among Republicans.

It was during the Republican administration of William McKinley that Hawai'i's destiny was decided. The case for annexing Hawai'i became part of the greater question of the Spanish-American War of 1898. Spain's colonial empire included the Philippines, and in the excitement of discovering a new political and strategic role for the United States in the Pacific, the annexation of Hawai'i, the key to the northern Pacific, became assured. By a joint resolution of Congress, successfully completed on July 7, 1898, Hawai'i was annexed. The Stars and Stripes was hoisted in the islands on August 12, 1898. Sanford Dole, the revolutionary who became President of the Hawaiian Republic, became the first governor of the territory of Hawai'i, when the new organic laws took effect in 1900.

U.S. TERRITORY

The revolution of 1893 and the annexation movement that followed are often referred to as nothing but products of the Hawaiian sugar industry. Certainly, there were the closest of associations between the men who owned and administered the sugar plantations and the men who organized and carried through the revolution. And just as certainly, the most substantial tie between Hawaiʻi and the United States, of an economic kind at least, was the one brought into being and maintained by the sugar industry.

This kind of simple explanation, however, neglects other important, perhaps crucial, factors. The style of government of the Kalākaua dynasty was distasteful to Americans in the islands on grounds other than purely economic. Revolutionaries from 1887 on saw themselves more as "good government men" than as mere self-interested sugar men. And, the annexationists of the 1890s regarded themselves far more strongly as American patriots, devotedly helping to work out the Manifest Destiny of their parent nation, than as men in isolation from their homeland, working out a narrow local economic interest.

Indeed, it was not the undivided opinion of white men in the islands that annexation to the United States would be good for Hawaiian sugar. To be sure, Hawaiʻi as American soil would not have the continuous worry over the American sugar tariff policy that Hawaiʻi as a foreign country had had. But then Hawaiʻi as American soil would necessarily fall under American legal control, and this, in the circumstances, might very well turn out to be disadvantageous to the cost structure of the island plantation companies. To be specific, Hawaiʻi as American soil would be subject to national controls on immigration. And at the turn of the century, opinion on the mainland was hardening discernibly against the continued admission of Asian immigrants, the very people upon whose continued presence in great numbers the sugar industry of the islands depended absolutely for survival.

As annexation became more and more

a practical possibility in the 1890s, the plantation owners hurried to bring in as many Asian laborers as they could in advance of any prospective prohibition. Most of the workers came from Japan. After the false start in 1868, importation of Japanese laborers began in earnest in 1887 and became more and more significant thereafter. By the year 1900, when American law became definitive in Hawaiʻi, there were more than 60,000 Japanese in the islands. In 1907 the United States, under the so-called Gentlemen's Agreement with the government of Japan, called a formal halt to the bringing in of Japanese. But even after that, more Japanese, many of them women, continued to be admitted to Hawaiʻi until 1924, when national immigration policy was hardened, stopping the flow almost completely. By 1920, 42.7% of the population of Hawaiian Islands was Japanese.

Even the Japanese, readily available as they

Children of Hawaiʻi on Annexation Day, 1898

were, proved not sufficient in numbers to keep Hawai'i's plantations fully staffed. Looking for a useful supplementary source, the plantation companies found one in the Philippines. In terms of immigration policy, the Philippines had the useful attribute of being under American control—they had passed from Spain to the hands of the United States as a result of the Spanish-American War of 1898. Between 1907 and the start of World War Two, more than 100,000 Filipinos, the overwhelming majority of them men, were imported as plantation laborers. Altogether the major groups of immigrants—Chinese, Japanese, Filipinos—and smaller contingents of Koreans, Portuguese, Spaniards, Russians, and other immigrants added a total of something like 400,000 to the statistics of population increase in Hawai'i. By no means did all of them stay in the islands, but enough did to create a new population.

Thus, in the long run, the labor policy of the plantation companies became the population policy of the islands. In terms of economics, Hawai'i was in the hands of the men who ran the sugar industry (and its associated industry, the growing and canning of pineapples, which became increasingly important in the twentieth century, emerging as a money-earner second only to sugar). Economic power was overwhelmingly centralized in the hands of five major companies, whose fortunes, founded on sugar, grew with the expanding and diversifying economy of the islands: Castle and Cooke, Alexander and Baldwin, C. Brewer, American Factors, and Theo H. Davies. A sixth major company, the Dillingham Corporation, was not a sugar house but matched the other five in size and influence during the period before World War Two. The political arrangements of the islands flowed from the economic arrangements. In general the prevailing view of politics in Hawai'i depended on the maintenance of Hawai'i as one big plantation, with a hierarchy of labor organized by race and nationality, so that Asians remained in the fields and the mills, leaving management and ownership to white men. In essence this economic, social, and political structure remained constant in Hawai'i from the start of the twentieth century to World War Two. Elections were dominated by the Republican Party, the party of property. It was, in its leadership at least, a party of white men, and it had the support of the Hawaiian and part-Hawaiian population, in what amounted to an anti-Asian alliance.

In the early decades of Hawai'i's life as a territory of the United States, the maintenance of these structures presented no great problems because, although the immigrants as a group dominated the population figures, they were aliens ineligible for citizenship and therefore ineligible to vote in elections.

By the same token, however, the Asian population could be seen as a force in politics in the not too distant future because the second generation, children of immigrant parents, born in the islands, would be Americans by birth and thus entitled to all the freedoms and responsibilities of citizenship, including the vote.

Particularly during the 1920s and 1930s, the matter of Americanization of the Asian emerged as a great and controversial topic of political argument and experimentation.

The situation was nothing if not complex. The first generation of Asians, the immigrants, not unnaturally kept quite close cultural and even political ties with their homelands. To perpetuate these ties, they set up churches, schools, newspapers, community associations, and other institutions. Not unnaturally as well, they wanted to see their children brought up as far as possible within the old cultural traditions. And yet by law and by residence, the children were Americans as well as Asians, members of American society as well as members of immigrant families.

The institution which provoked the greatest amount of heated argument and governmental intervention was the language school. Chinese and Japanese children educated in the public schools often went after regular school hours for a supplementary education in the language, religion, and culture of their parents' homeland. The most determined Americanizers in the white community of Hawai'i came to believe

Pearl Harbor about 1880

December 7, 1941

that these schools, as long as they were allowed to continue to exist, would present insuperable obstacles to the social assimilation of the young Asians. Eventually legislation was passed against the schools in the territorial legislature. Lawsuits followed, and the issue was fought all the way up to the United States Supreme Court, where in 1927 a judgment was handed down affirming the legality and constitutionality of the language schools. They continued to operate.

The Supreme Court judgment caused the Americanizers even more dissatisfaction. Their anxiety and concern about the immigrant population and its American offspring increased markedly during the 1930s. By this time, the question had ceased to be merely a local one, limited in its implications to Hawai'i. The Japanese had emerged as the biggest single group in the population of the islands at the same time as the Japanese Empire was emerging as a political and military threat to the interests of the United States in the Pacific.

By the mid-1930s, Hawai'i seemed as precariously placed as it had ever been. It was the forward base of the American armed forces in the Pacific, with Pearl Harbor highly developed as the home of the Pacific Fleet, and Schofield Barracks in central O'ahu the biggest Army installation in the nation—and all this in a place where people of Japanese ancestry formed the biggest single identifiable portion of the population.

The question of the loyalty of Hawai'i's Japanese population in the case of war was problematic. It could only be resolved by war.

PEARL HARBOR

At 7:55 a.m. on Sunday, December 7, 1941, carrier-based fighters and bombers of the Japanese Empire attacked Pearl Harbor and other military installations on O'ahu, sinking a number of battleships and other heavy vessels, and inflicting in one morning the worst damage to American armed strength in the history of the nation.

Martial law was declared in the islands on Pearl Harbor day and remained in effect until late in the war, despite the vigorous efforts of some members of the civilian administration to have it lifted after the theater of conflict in the Pacific moved farther and farther west, away from Hawai'i, as the tide of battle turned.

To begin, in the hours that followed the attack on Pearl Harbor, the entire Japanese population of Hawai'i, about 160,000, was under suspicion of complicity, and there were tense days before it became clear that the first devastating attack was not to be followed by invasion.

Among the Japanese community, a number of Buddhist and Shinto priests, language teachers, newspaper editors, and other leading figures were arrested and interned, first in Hawai'i, then on the mainland—in all, less than one percent of the Japanese in Hawai'i. Investigations during and after the war by the FBI and other agencies confirmed that no Hawai'i Japanese was guilty of espionage or sabotage.

For the younger Japanese, those born in the islands, the great test of loyalty was to fight under the American flag. Those who wanted the opportunity were at first denied it. The armed forces would not take them as recruits. After a year of war, the Army reconsidered, and an all-Japanese volunteer unit was formed. First as the 100th Battalion, then as the 442nd Regimental Combat Team, the young Japanese, *nisei* in their parents' language, Americans of Japanese ancestry by their own designation, fought with great distinction in the European theater. They became the most highly decorated unit in the United States armed forces.

The war changed Hawaiian society irreversibly. There was no chance that after 1945 things would revert to their pre-war condition. The most easily visible sign was that the Asian population became politically active and influential. This movement was led to a large extent by war veterans, including many members of the 442nd, who went on to college after the war on the GI Bill, and then took a law degree and went into politics. Given the domination of the islands by the Republican Party in the great days of the plantation society, it was predictable that the new generation of Asian politicians and voters would attach themselves for the most part to the Democratic Party. After the first few years of organization in the post-war period, the Democratic Party established itself as a genuinely multi-racial organization, broadly based on the diverse population of the islands. This became, in turn, its guarantee of success at the polls. By 1954, with Republicans in power nationally, the Democrats became the party of power in Hawai'i. They were able to remain in power through the rest of the 1950s and all through the 1960s.

Contemporary with the rise of the Democratic Party, and connected with it in many ways, was the rise of an organized labor movement in the islands. This again was part of a great social transformation. As early as the beginning of the twentieth century, there had been strikes on the plantations from time to time, some of them long and bitter, involving thousands of workers. To handle the labor problem, the plantation companies used a mixture of methods, ranging from the introduction of strike-breaking workers to strategically timed sensible and humane concessions. Compared with the situation on the American mainland, the life of an agricultural laborer on a Hawaiian plantation was by no means bad, and it compared favorably even with the life of a good many mainland industrial workers. This comparison, of course, was not one made by the workers themselves, and when it was brought to their attention, it did not make them any less interested in labor organizations, which may have brought further improvements.

If the labor movement was not quick to grow to a position of strength, this was due principally to the mixed racial and national origins of the work force of the plantations. Communication and cooperation were difficult between native Hawaiians and part-Hawaiians, Chinese, Japanese, and Filipinos. All the plantation strikes before World War Two were mounted by workers organized according to nationality, and this meant that there was no industry-wide workers' program of any significance.

The modern labor movement got definitively under way with the passage by Congress in 1935 of the National Labor Relations Act and the affirmation of its constitutionality by a decision of the Supreme Court in 1937. This opened the way for systematic organization of unions in Hawai'i as elsewhere in the nation. A good deal

Lei Lady

depended, in the case of the mechanized plantations of Hawai'i, on having workers classified for organizational purposes as industrial rather than agricultural because the national legislation was aimed at factories rather than farms. Decisions of the National Labor Relations Board favored industrial classification for the great bulk of Hawai'i's plantation workers, and with this established, the organization could go ahead with every prospect of substantial success.

The first successful union organizers were men who had experience in the maritime unions of the American west coast, and in fact organization in Hawai'i was begun on

politics vigorously, and during the early years of its post-war activities, it sometimes seemed on the brink of taking over the Democratic Party altogether. This never happened, but then and later, endorsement by organized labor was regarded as a considerable asset to a political candidate.

In the course of establishing its dominant position in the post-war years, the ILWU, under its leader Jack Hall, called several major strikes on the plantations, and an extremely long and bitter one on the waterfront in 1949. As virtually all of Hawai'i's commerce was seaborne, this was tantamount to bringing the economy to a

STATEHOOD CELEBRATION

The question of Communism became a stumbling block to the realization of the great ambition of businessmen in the islands: to see Hawai'i admitted to the union of states. Since Hawai'i became a territory in 1900, there had been periodical review on its status. The political arrangement had been satisfactory enough to begin with, but with the passing of the years, it became less and less so. By the 1950s, Hawai'i's population was larger than that of several states at the time of their admission. Its tax payments to the federal treasury were likewise larger than

On August 21, 1959 Hawai'i was admitted to the Union as the Fiftieth State.

the waterfront, spreading from there to the plantations. The International Longshoremen's and Warehousemen's Union emerged as the chief spokesman of the workers and had just succeeded in writing the first sizeable contracts with management when World War Two broke out.

Labor organization was effectively brought to a halt during the war under martial law, with its restrictions on civil liberty and industrial mobility. But after peace returned, the same forces, which brought the Democratic Party to a position of strength at the polls, created a labor movement which could number its members in the tens of thousands. The ILWU went into

standstill—evidence of the tremendous power organized labor had come to wield.

The tactics of the ILWU were undoubtedly extreme, too much so for a good many Democratic politicians, certainly so for almost all Republicans. Some of the union leaders came out of the Marxist-oriented maritime unions of the 1930s. These facts, considered in the general climate of the Cold War of the early 1950s, led to several investigations of Communism in Hawai'i by Congressional committees. The upshot was that in 1953 Jack Hall and six others, among them some Asians, were tried and convicted under the Smith Act (their convictions were eventually reversed on appeal).

those of several states. It had been a territory for longer than any other before admission. Under the law of the territory, framed by Congress, the voters of Hawai'i did not elect their own governor, and their most important judges were presidential appointees. Their single elected representative in Congress had a voice but no vote. Congress could still alter at will the sugar legislation crucial to Hawai'i and had indeed done so for a short time in the 1930s. Congress in fact could alter the form of government of the islands, and this had taken place when martial law was imposed after the attack on Pearl Harbor.

Once again, it was the experience of

World War Two that got a sustained statehood movement under way. The feeling of a majority of people in the islands was that the war record of the people of Hawai'i, from Pearl Harbor to V-J Day, was that of people who deserved to be regarded as first-class citizens. Their loyalty to the United States could not sensibly be regarded as deficient. Statehood should be theirs, as a matter of justice, as a matter of right.

In fact, the first congressional hearings on the subject of statehood for Hawai'i were held as early as 1935, but it was not until 1959 that the matter was finally resolved.

The idea of statehood for Hawai'i took a long time to gain authority in Washington. Hearings multiplied, legislation was framed and discussed but never passed. In a sense, the argu-ments over statehood were not much more than a repetition of the debate over the annexation of Hawai'i in 1898. To some congressmen, and particularly to some Southern senators, the fact that Hawai'i was distant from the mainland, and that its population was mixed and getting more so with each generation, seemed to argue against admitting the islands as a state on the basis of equality with other states. Newer issues were added to this old one. The power of the labor unions was deplored. It was alleged that Communists dominated the government and society of the territory. Such assertions, rebut-tals, claims, and counterclaims about the real nature of society in Hawai'i kept the issue alive throughout the 1950s.

Not until 1959 did Congressional Delegate John Burns and the other leaders of the state-hood movement taste success. On several ear-lier occasions, Congress had arrived at the point of giving serious consideration to a statehood bill, but it had never been possible to maneuver a bill through both houses. Now the best oppor-tunity of all arose. Alaska was being considered for statehood at the same time, and a strategy of permitting Alaska to become the 49th state was developed. Once this was accomplished, the logic and reasonability of admitting Hawai'i were clear to all who mattered, and passage of the necessary legislation was assured. On March 11, 1959, the Senate passed a statehood bill; the House followed suit on March 12; a plebiscite in Hawai'i produced a majority in favor of admis-sion of 17 to 1; and on Admission Day, August 21, 1959, Hawai'i became the 50th state.

Like reciprocity and annexation before it, this new attachment to the nation brought with it an economic boom. In the decade that followed statehood, Hawai'i became populous and prosperous as never before. The economic base changed: sugar and pineapple were supplemented and finally supplanted as prime money earners by tourism and federal spending, the bulk of the latter military in application. The jet plane, which was the making of the tourist industry, encouraged closer connections between Hawai'i and the mainland, and this in turn influenced a new kind of migration to Hawai'i: mainland Americans, who by the end of the 1960s, were arriving in such numbers to take up residence that a future was foreseeable in which a situation new to Hawai'i in the twentieth century would develop—one ethnic group would comprise an absolute majority of the population. Increasingly, the style of life of the islands was assimilated to that of the mainland. The passage from undiscovered islands to statehood had taken less than two hundred years.

Makaha Point
Kalalau
Hanalei
Kilauea
Kahala Point
Summit Camp
Mt. Waialeale
+5170
Kapaa
Mana
KAUAI
Lehua Island
Waimea
Lihue
Kii Landing
1281
Paniau
Koloa
Puuwai
NIIHAU
Keelinawi
Keanahaki Bay
Hanapepe Bay
Kaula
Kaulakahi Channel
Kauai Channel

Kahuku Point
Waimea
Kahuku
Kaena Point
Waialua
Kahana
4046+
Wahiawa
Waianae
OAHU
Waipahu
Kaneol
Kai
+3150
Barbers Point
Pearl Harbor
Honolulu
Ku
Diamond Head

Kure Island
(Ocean I.)
Midway Islands
Seal Island
Southeast I.
Salmon Bank
Pioneer Bank
Lisianski Island
Laysan Island
Raita Bank
Maro Reef
Gardner Pinnacles
St. Rogatien Bank
Tern Island
La Perouse Pinnacle
Necker Island
Disappearing I.
French Frigate Shoals
Nihoa

THE HAWAIIAN CHAIN

ISLAND	AREA IN SQUARE MILES
Hawaii	4,021
Maui	728
Oahu	595
Kauai	551
Molokai	259
Lanai	141
Niihau	72
Kahoolawe	45
Northwest Islets	3
TOTAL	6,415

26°
24°

NIIHAU
Kaula
KAUAI
OAHU
MOLOKAI
LANAI
MAUI
KAHOOLAWE
20°

HAWAII

0   100   200   300
STATUTE MILES

176°   172°   168°   164°   160°   156°

160°   159°   158°

The Principal
HAWAIIAN ISLANDS

0   25   50
STATUTE MILES

MAP SYMBOLS

——— Roads

═══ Dual Lane Roads

----- Trails

(69) Highway Numbers

(HI) Interstate

✈ Commercial Airfields

✈ Military Airfields

Coral Reef

Swamp

← Warm Currents

Elevations in Feet

Special Points of Interest

□ Other Points of Interest

Heiau (Ancient Temple)

Petroglyphs (Rock Paintings)

∴ Ruins

MOLOKAI

Ilio Point
Moomomi
ouhi
Kalaupapa
na Loa
+1381
Hoolehua
Halawa
4970+
Kaunakakai
Pukoo
Kamalo

Pailolo Channel

LANAI

Pohakuloa Pt.
Kaena Point
+1799
Lanai City
+3370
Kaumalapau
Palaoa Point
Manele Bay

KAHOOLAWE
Kukui Point
+1477

MAUI

Honokohau
Kaanapali
Nailuku
Pauwela
5788+
Kailua
Lahaina
Kahului
Olowalu
Honomaele
Waiakoa
Red Hill
Kamaole
10023+
Hana
Nuu
Koali
Keoneoio

Alenuihaha Channel

HAWAII

Upolu Point
Hawi
Kohala
Mahukona
Waipio
Kukuihaele
Honokaa
Kawaihae
5505+
Paauilo
Waimea
(Kamuela)
Laupahoehoe
Hakalau
Kiholo
Mauna Kea
+13796
Papaikou
Puuanahulu
Pohakuloa
Hilo
Mahaiula
Keaau (Olaa)
Kailua
Mountain View
Kainaliu
Mauna Loa
Pahoa
Kealakekua
+13680
Pohoiki
Kilauea Crater
Honaunau
4077+
Kalapana
Koa Mill
Milolii
Pahala
Ninole
Waiohinu
Naalehu
Ka Lae (South Point)

Original map was created in 1970.

22°

21°

20°

19°

157°   156°   155°   154°

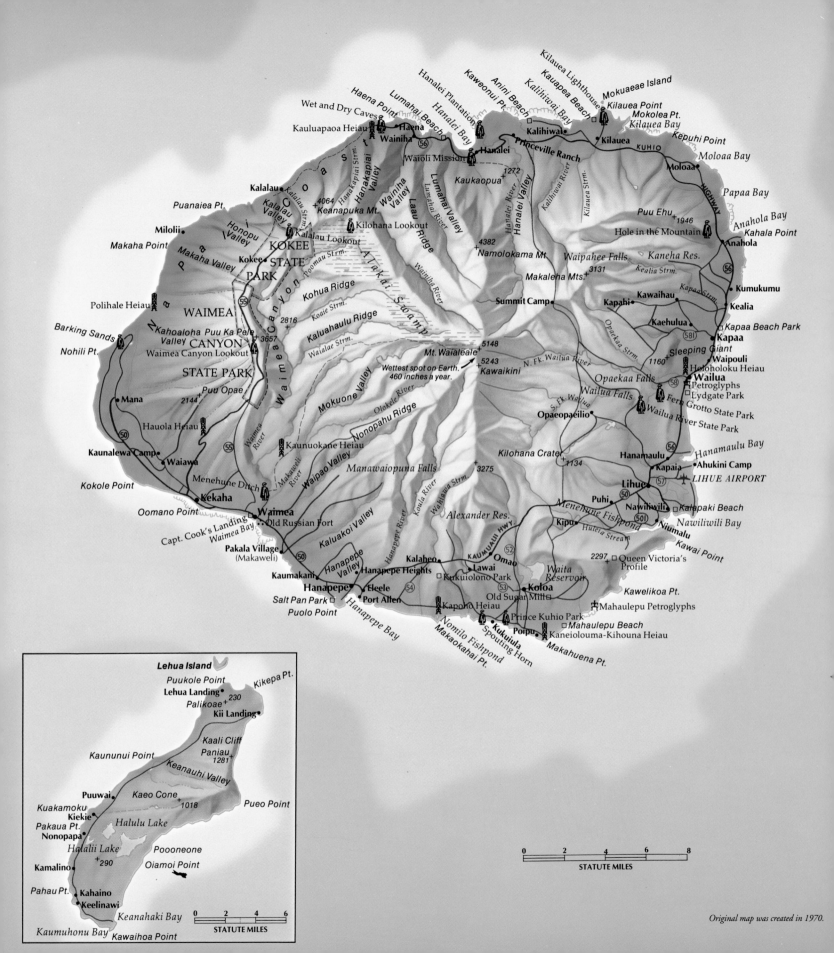

Kilauea Lighthouse
Kauapea Beach
Mokuaeae Island
Kilauea Point
Mokolea Pt.
Kilauea Bay
Kilauea
Kepuhi Point
KUHIO
Moloaa Bay
Moloaa
HIGHWAY
Papaa Bay
Puu Ehu +1946
Hole in the Mountain
Anahola Bay
Kahala Point
Anahola
Kaneha Res.
Waipahee Falls
56
Kealia Strm.
3131
Kumukumu
Kealia
Kapaa Strm.
Kawaihau
Kapahi
Kapaa Beach Park
Kaehulua
581
Kapaa
Sleeping Giant
Waipouli
Opaekaa Strm.
1160
Holoholoku Heiau
Sleeping Giant
Wailua
Opaekaa Falls
58
Petroglyphs
Wailua Falls
Lydgate Park
Opaeopaeilio
Fern Grotto State Park
S. Fk. Wailua
Wailua River State Park
N. Fk. Wailua River
56
Hanamaulu Bay
Kilohana Crater +1134
Hanamaulu
Ahukini Camp
Kapaia
LIHUE AIRPORT
Lihue
57
Puhi
Nawiliwili
50
Kalapaki Beach
Menehune Fishpond
501
Niumalu
Nawiliwili Bay
Kipu
Hulela Stream
Kawai Point
2297
Queen Victoria's Profile
Alexander Res.
KAUMUALII HWY.
52
Waita Reservoir
Omao
Kalaheo
Kawelikoa Pt.
Lawai
53
Mahaulepu Petroglyphs
Kukuiolono Park
Koloa
Old Sugar Mill
Kapoho Heiau
Prince Kuhio Park
Mahaulepu Beach
Nomilo Fishpond
Kukuiula
Poipu
Kaneiolouma-Kihouna Heiau
Spouting Horn
Makaokahai Pt.
Makahuena Pt.

Wet and Dry Caves
Haena Point
Lumahai Beach
Haena
Kauluapaoa Heiau
Wainiha
Hanalei Point
Hanalei Plantation
Kaweonui Pt.
Anini Beach
Kalihiwai Bay
Kalihiwai
Kalihiwai
Princeville Ranch
Waioli Mission
Hanalei
Hanalei Bay
Kaukaopua
1272
Kalalau
Puanaiea Pt.
Milolii
Kalalau Valley
4064
Keanapuka Mt.
Kilohana Lookout
Kalalau Lookout
Hanakapiai Valley
Hanakoa Strm.
Wainiha Valley
Lumahai Valley
Lumahai River
Wainiha River
Laau Ridge
Kalihiwai River
Hanalei River
Hanalei Valley
Kilauea Strm.
Kohua Ridge
KOKEE STATE PARK
Kokee
Makaha Point
Makaha Valley
Namolokama Mt.
4382
Makaleha Mts.
Summit Camp
Kaluahaulu Ridge
2816
Koaie Strm.
Waialae Strm.
Alakai Swamp
Mt. Waialeale +5148
Wettest spot on Earth.
460 inches a year.
5243
Kawaikini
Barking Sands
Polihale Heiau
WAIMEA
Kahoaloha Puu Ka Pele
Valley
CANYON
3657
Nohili Pt.
Waimea Canyon Lookout
STATE PARK
Puu Opae
Mokuone Valley
Waimea Canyon
Poomau Strm.
Nonopahu Ridge
Olokele River
Manawaiopuna Falls
Koula River
Waihawa Strm.
3275
Mana
2144
Hauola Heiau
Kaunuokane Heiau
Waipao Valley
Makaweli River
Kaunalewa Camp
Waiawa
Kokole Point
Menehune Ditch
Kekaha
Kaluakoi Valley
Oomano Point
Waimea
Old Russian Fort
Capt. Cook's Landing
Waimea Bay
Pakala Village
(Makaweli)
50
Kaumakani
Hanapepe Valley
Hanapepe Heights
Kalaheo
Kaumakani
Hanapepe
Eleele
54
Kukuiolono Park
Salt Pan Park
Port Allen
Puolo Point
Hanapepe Bay

STATUTE MILES
0   2   4   6   8

Original map was created in 1970.

Lehua Island
Puukole Point
Kikepa Pt.
Lehua Landing
230
Palikoae +
Kii Landing
Kaali Cliff
Paniau
Kaunauhi Valley
1281
Kaununui Point
Puuwai
Kaeo Cone +
1018
Pueo Point
Kuakamoku
Kiekie
Pakaua Pt.
Nonopapa
Halulu Lake
Kamalino
Halalii Lake
Poooneone
290
Oiamoi Point
Pahau Pt.
Kahaino
Keelinawi
Keanahaki Bay
Kaumuhonu Bay
Kawaihoa Point

STATUTE MILES
0   2   4   6

KAUA'I AND NI'IHAU

Kaua'i, the people of old believed, is the eldest of the twelve children born to Wākea, the Sky God, and Papa, the Earth Mother. Despite her age, Kaua'i is "beautiful beyond compare." Romantic newcomers in the Nineteenth Century called Kaua'i "The Garden Isle." A single volcano made this island: Wai'ale'ale's high, curved rampart is the eastern rim of the huge caldera, the largest in the Hawaiian Chain. Erosion has filled the caldera almost to its brim and has carved deep valleys in its flanks.

Ni'ihau, purchased from King Kamehameha V in 1864 by Mrs. Elizabeth Sinclair, is owned by her descendants, the Robinson family of Kaua'i. Ni'ihau's several hundred residents, almost all of who are Hawaiians or part-Hawaiians, now live there only in summer, and otherwise attend school and work on Kaua'i.

1
LĪHU'E is the capital of Kaua'i County (which includes Ni'ihau). In 2007 the income of Kaua'i's 62,828 residents came from tourism and agriculture.

2
WAIMEA CANYON, a miniature Grand Canyon of the Colorado, is 10 miles long, 2,857 feet deep at its highest point.

3
WAIMEA Captain James Cook and members of his exploring expedition, who discovered these islands on January 18, 1778, made their first landing at Waimea two days later.

4
MENEHUNE DITCH About a mile inland, on Waimea River's western bank, a short section of this ancient stonework still helps to irrigate the taro patches.

5
FORT ELIZABETH Just east of Waimea, at the river's mouth, lie the ruins of Fort Elizabeth, a trading post and fortress built by Russian funding in 1815-1816.

6
MOUNT WAI'ALE'ALE, 5,240 feet high, is considered to be the world's "rainiest spot." Average annual rainfall is 486 inches.

7
KŌLOA Hawai'i's first successful sugar plantation was started at Kōloa in 1835.

8
HĀ'UPU RIDGE German immigrants explained the name of east Kaua'i's seaport by pointing to Hā'upu Ridge. There, in basalt sculptured by wind and rain, matronly Queen Victoria lifts a reproving finger to her nephew Kaiser Wilhelm, saying, "Now, Willy, Willy," (Nawiliwili, the name of the nearby port).

9
WAILUA VALLEY The ruins of many ancient temples can be found in Wailua Valley, once the residence of Kaua'i's kings. Best preserved are Holoholokū heiau and the royal birthstones.

10
NĀ PALI COAST You can see some of these spectacular cliffs if you'll walk about a hundred yards along the trail which begins at Hā'ena.

11
KALALAU VALLEY Don't miss the view of Kalalau Valley from the lookout near Kōke'e, 4,000 feet above the distant sea.

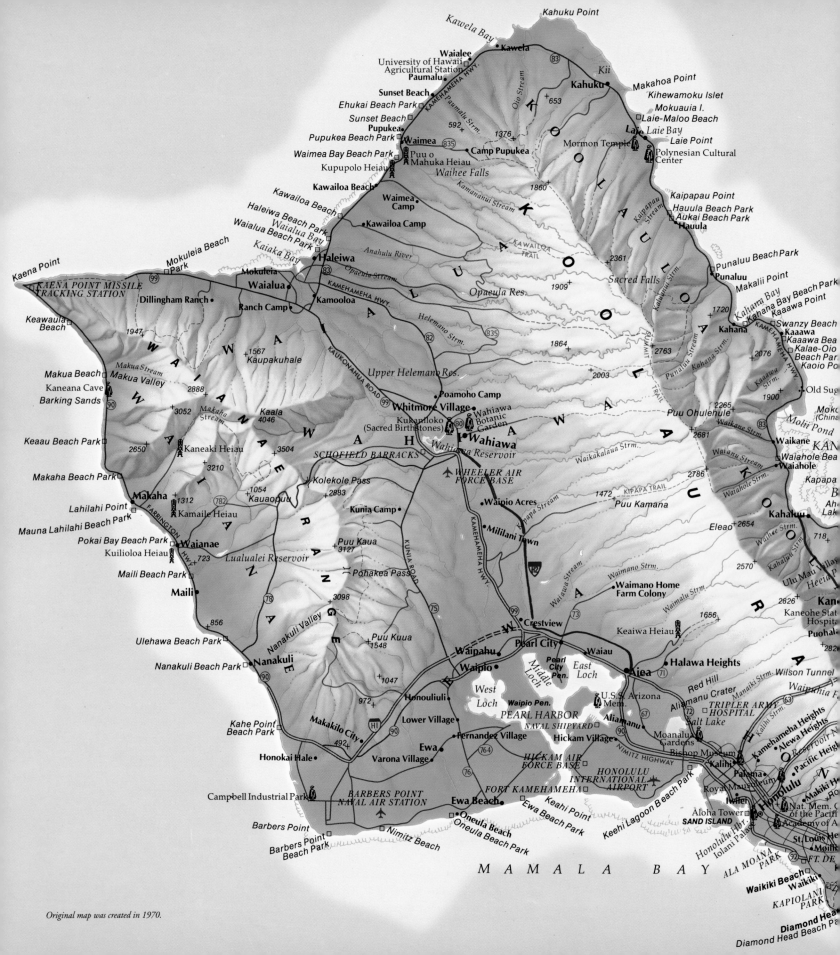

Kahuku Point

Kawela Bay
Waialee   Kawela
University of Hawaii
Agricultural Station
Paumalu   Kii
Kahuku
Makahoa Point
Kihewamoku Islet
Sunset Beach
Ehukai Beach Park   653
Sunset Beach   592   1376
Pupukea   Mokuauia I.
Pupukea Beach Park   Waimea
Waimea Bay Beach Park   Puu o
Kupupolo Heiau   Mahuka Heiau
Camp Pupukea
Waihee Falls

Laie-Maloo Beach
Laie   Laie Bay
Mormon Temple   Laie Point
Polynesian Cultural
Center

Kawailoa Beach   1860
Kawailoa Beach
Haleiwa Beach Park   Waimea
Waialua Bay   Camp
Waialua Beach Park
Kaiaka Bay   Kawailoa Camp

Kaipapau Point
Hauula Beach Park
Aukai Beach Park
Hauula

Mokuleia Beach
Park   Haleiwa
Kaena Point   Mokuleia
Waialua   Anahulu River
KAENA POINT MISSILE   Kamooloa
TRACKING STATION
Keawaula   Dillingham Ranch   Ranch Camp
Beach

Opaeula Res.   1909
Sacred Falls   2361
Punaluu Beach Park
Punaluu
Makalii Point
1720   Kahana Bay
Kahana Bay Beach Park
Kaaawa Point

Makua Beach   1947
Kaneana Cave   Makua Valley
Barking Sands   Makua Stream
Keaau Beach Park   2888   3052
Makaha Stream   Kaala   4046
Kaneaki Heiau   3504
Makaha Beach Park   2650   3210
Makaha   1312   1054
Lahilahi Point   Kamaile Heiau   2883
Mauna Lahilahi Beach Park   Kauaopuu
Pokai Bay Beach Park   Waianae
Kuilioloa Heiau   723
Maili Beach Park   Lualualei Reservoir
Maili

Kaupakuhale   1567
Upper Helemano Res.
Poamoho Camp
Whitmore Village
Kukaniloko   Wahiawa
(Sacred Birthstones)   Botanic Garden
Wahiawa
SCHOFIELD BARRACKS   Wahiawa Reservoir
Kolekole Pass   WHEELER AIR
FORCE BASE
Kunia Camp   Waipio Acres
Puu Kaua   3127
Mililani Town
Pohakea Pass
3098

Helemano Strm.
1864   2003
Kawailoa Trail   Puu Ohulehule
2763   2681   2265
2786
KIPAPA TRAIL   1472
Puu Kamana
1900
Old Sug
Molii Pond
Waikane
Waiahole Bea
Waiahole
Kapapa

Swanzy Beach
Kaaawa
Kaaawa Bea
Kalae-Oio
Beach Par
Kaoio Po

Nanakuli Valley   Puu Kuua   1548
Ulehawa Beach Park   856
Nanakuli   1047
Nanakuli Beach Park   972
Honouliuli
Kahe Point   Makakilo City   Lower Village
Beach Park   492
Honokai Hale
Campbell Industrial Park   BARBERS POINT
NAVAL AIR STATION
Barbers Point
Barbers Point
Beach Park

Kahaluu
Eleao   2654
2570   718
1656   2826
Waimano Home   Kan
Farm Colony   Kaneohe Stat
Keaiwa Heiau   Hospita
Crestview   Puohai
Waipahu   Pearl City   Waiau
Waipio   Aiea   Halawa Heights
West   Pearl   East   Wilson Tunnel
Loch   City   Loch   Red Hill
Pen.   Aliamanu Crater
Middle   U.S.S. Arizona   TRIPLER ARMY
Loch   Mem.   HOSPITAL
Waipio Pen.   Salt Lake
PEARL HARBOR   Aliamanu
NAVAL SHIPYARD   Moanalua
Fernandez Village   Gardens   Bishop Museum
Ewa   Hickam Village   Kalihi
Varona Village   HICKAM AIR   HONOLULU   Palama
FORCE BASE   INTERNATIONAL   Iwilei
FORT KAMEHAMEHA   AIRPORT
Ewa Beach   Keahi Point   Royal Maus
Oneula Beach   Keehi Point   Aloha Tower
Oneula Beach Park   Ewa Beach Park   Keehi Lagoon Beach Park   St
Nimitz Beach   SAND ISLAND   Iolani Pala

Kamehameha Heights
Alewa Heights
Reservoir
Pacific Heig
Maki Hi
Maki
Nat. Mem.
of the Pacific
Academy of

MAMALA BAY
Waikiki Beach   Waikiki
KAPIOLANI
PARK
Diamond Hea
Diamond Head Beach Park

Original map was created in 1970.

O'AHU

O'ahu means "The Gathering Place." The little port on its southern shore, the only protected harbor in all Hawai'i, drew foreigners and their ships to Honolulu, making it the Crossroads of the Pacific and the major portal of entry for people and their possessions coming to these islands.

This island is about 40 miles long and 26 miles wide and has an area of 595 square miles. About 905,601 people live on the island this year, each having two to three cars per household. Major sources of income are tourists, military establishments, agencies of federal, state, and county governments, and the innumerable service industries concerned in maintaining the state's residents and visitors. The last pineapple harvest was in 2008.

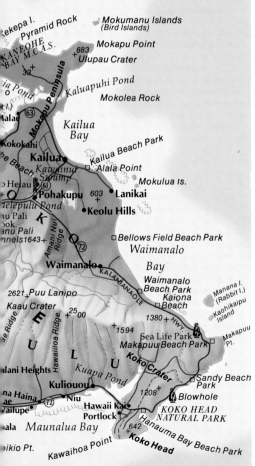

1

WAI'ANAE MOUNTAINS in the west and the Ko'olau Mountains in the east are the remnants of the two great volcanoes which made O'ahu.

2

'IOLANI PALACE, a symbol of old Hawai'i, was restored in 1978. Built for King Kalākaua in 1879-1881, and used after the monarchy as an office building, it is now a museum open to the public.

3

BERNICE P. BISHOP MUSEUM, founded in 1889, is the primary repository for relics of Hawai'i's past. Its research programs are concerned with Polynesia's past, present, and future.

4

PUNCHBOWL In the crater of Punchbowl, once called Pu'u o waina, Hill of Sacrifice, the remains of American soldiers, sailors, and marines lie in the National Memorial Cemetery of the Pacific.

5

SEA LIFE PARK, near Makapu'u Point, exhibits living creatures from the sea. At adjacent Oceanic Institute, marine biologists study them.

6

USS ARIZONA MEMORIAL The United States Navy offers an instructive tour of the USS Arizona Memorial, dedicated to victims of Japan's attack upon Pearl Harbor on December 7, 1941.

Ilio Point
Mokio Point
Waiakanapo
658+
Kaiehu Point
Kepuhi
Moomomi
Papohaku Beach
Wahilauhue
Kakaako Gulch
Kahanui Gulch
Anahaki Gulch
48
Papa Gulch
Palaau State Park
Hoolehua
MOLOKAI AIRPORT
Kalae
Mahana
46
Puu Nana
1381
Kualapuu
Wahilauhue Gulch
Waiakane Gulch
Kaunalu Bay
Kahea Gulch
811
Mauna Loa
133
46
47
Kalamaula Village
Kaulahuki
3753
Llaau Pt.
Hakina Gulch
Kolo
Umipaa
Kaunakaki Gulch
Halena
Home of Kamehameha V
Kaunakakai
Kamiloloa
45
Kaunakakai Harbor
Black Rock
Moku
Kawela
City of Refuge
Hale o Lono Pt.
Kahiu Point
Kalaupapa Lighthouse
Kuahu Heiau
Makanalua Peninsula
Kaunako Crater
Kalaupapa
Father Damien's Church
Mokapu Island
Leinaopapio Pt.
Kalawao
Ahina Heiau
Kalawao
Haupu Bay
Pelekunu Bay
Kaaiku Heiau
Wahilanau Strm.
Waikolu Strm.
4602
Malahini Cave
4970
Kamakou
Wailua Stream
Kikipua Point
Papalaua Falls
Wailau
Hipuapua Falls
Papa Heiau
Halawa Strm.
Kahoonoho Heiau
1552
Moaula Falls
Lamaloa
Halawa
Halawa
Mok
1538
Waialua Stream
45
Waialua
Iliiliopae Heiau
Pauwalu
Hokukano Heiau
Pukoo
Malae Heiau
Kaluaaha
Kamalo
Ualapue
Kalaeloa Point
Kalaeloa Harbor
Pailolo Cha

K a l o h i   C h a n n e l

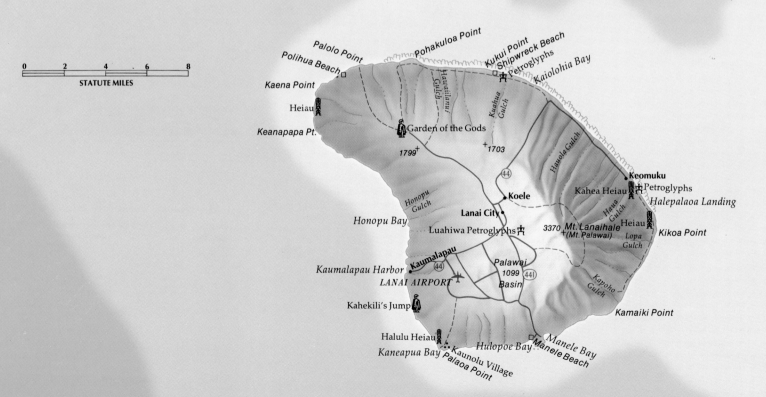

Palolo Point
Pohakuloa Point
Kukui Point
Shipwreck Beach
Polihua Beach
Petroglyphs
Kaiolohia Bay
Kaena Point
Hawaiilanui Gulch
Kuahua Gulch
Heiau
Garden of the Gods
1703
Keanapapa Pt.
1799
Honopu Gulch
44
Keomuku
Kahea Heiau
Petroglyphs
Halepalaoa Landing
Koele
Honopu Bay
Lanai City
Hauola Gulch
Luahiwa Petroglyphs
3370 Mt. Lanaihale
(Mt. Palawai)
Heiau
Kikoa Point
Hana Gulch
Lopa Gulch
Kaumalapau
44
Palawai
Kaumalapau Harbor
441
1099
Basin
Kapoho Gulch
LANAI AIRPORT
Kamaiki Point
Kahekili's Jump
Halulu Heiau
Manele Bay
Kaneapua Bay
Kaunolu Village
Hulopoe Bay
Manele Beach
Palaoa Point

0   2   4   6   8
STATUTE MILES

Original map was created in 1970.

MOLOKA'I AND LĀNA'I

Long ago Moloka'i, Lāna'i, and Maui were united in a single island. Since 1905 they have been jointed politically, to constitute Maui County. Lāna'i, however, is now owned by Castle & Cooke.

After the long body of Moloka'i had been produced by two major volcanoes, a little afterthought crater, midway in the northern escarpment, added the miniscule promontory of Kalaupapa. Upon this leaf of land, a settlement for Hawai'i's lepers has existed since 1886. Treatment for Hansen's Disease after World War Two changed people's attitudes toward patients, who were no longer required to live there. Today a national historical park in the area serves as a way to remember and to educate visitors. Kalaupapa is still home to former patients, as well as park employees.

More than 7,000 people live on Moloka'i, "The Friendly Island," working in diversified agriculture, or on their own homestead-farms.

In 1922 Dole Corporation's founder bought most of Lā na'i, "The Pineapple Island," from Maui's Baldwin family, for $1,100,000. Pineapple production was replaced by cattle farms in the late 20th century.

1
PHALLIC ROCK Proper maps do not show it, ~~s~~o ask a friendly islander where to find the most ~~u~~nabashed phallic rock in the United States.

2
FISHPONDS Along Moloka'i's southern coast are ~~s~~ome of the few surviving stone-walled fishponds ~~b~~uilt by aboriginal Hawaiians. Marine biologists ~~a~~re using these in experiments to increase yields of ~~f~~ood from the sea.

3
AT KALAWAO, Father Damien de Veuster ~~m~~inistered to afflicted patients from 1873 until he, ~~a~~ leper himself, died in 1889. The two conjoined ~~c~~hurches of St. Philomena and an empty grave are ~~h~~is memorials. His body was returned to Louvain, ~~B~~elgium, in 1936.

4
SILOAMA Between Kalawao and the former ~~l~~eprosarium at Kalaupapa is Siloama, the Church ~~o~~f the Healing Spring, a bit of Protestant New ~~E~~ngland transplanted to the tropics.

5
AXIS DEER, thriving in Moloka'i's wilderness, are fair game for hunters during prescribed periods. Islanders express divided opinions about the merits of releasing these deer upon the Big Island.

6
PINEAPPLES About 15,000 of Lānai's 90,200 acres were planted in pineapples. The land now supports high quality beef and game hunting.

7
KAUMALAPAU From Lānai's pocket harbor of Kaumalapau, harvested pineapples were shipped by barge to Dole Corporation's cannery in Honolulu, 60 nautical miles away.

8
PETROGLYPHS and rock platforms, on which natives built their grass huts, identify the ruins of several ancient villages on Lāna'i's windward coast.

9
NORFOLK ISLAND PINES, planted as windbreaks in and around Lāna'i City, also help to collect water from mist.

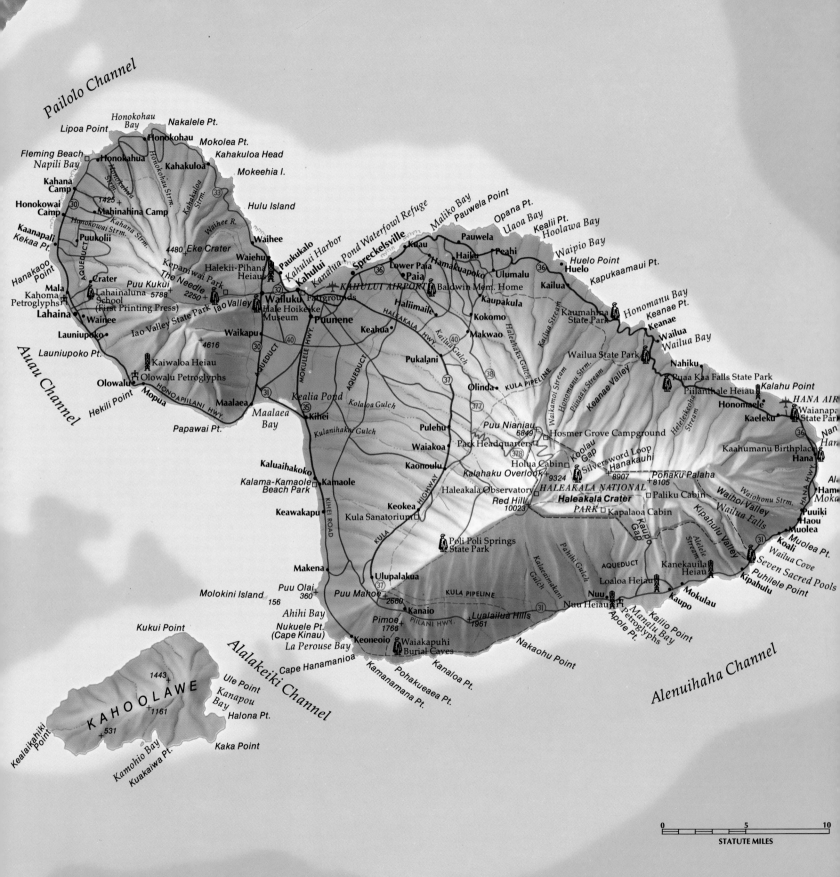

Pailolo Channel

Honokohau Bay
Lipoa Point
Nakalele Pt.
Honokohau
Mokolea Pt.
Fleming Beach
Napili Bay
Honokahua
Kahakuloa Head
Kahakuloa
Mokeehia I.
Kahana Camp
Honokowai Camp
Mahinahina Camp
1425
Kaanapali
Kekaa Pt.
Puukolii
Hulu Island
4480 Eke Crater
Waihee
Waihee R.
Hanakaoo Point
Crater
Puu Kukui
5788
The Needle
2250
Kepaniwai Park
Waiehu
Halekii-Pihana Heiaus
Paukukalo
Kahului Harbor
Kahului
Kanaha Pond Waterfowl Refuge
Maliko Bay
Pauwela Point
Opana Pt.
Uaoa Bay
Kealii Pt.
Hoolawa Bay
Waipio Bay
Spreckelsville
Lower Paia
Kuau
Pauwela
Haiku
Peahi
Huelo Point
Huelo
Kapukaamaui Pt.
Mala
Kahoma Petroglyphs
Lahainaluna School
(First Printing Press)
Iao Valley State Park
Hale Hoikeike Museum
Wailuku
Fairgrounds
KAHULUI AIRPORT
Baldwin Mem. Home
Kailua
Honomanu Bay
Keanae Pt.
Kaumahina State Park
Keanae
Lahaina
Wainee
Puunene
Haliimaile
Hamakuapoko
Ulumalu
Kaupakula
Kokomo
HALEAKALA HWY
Kailua Stream
Wailua
Wailua Bay
Launiupoko
Iao Valley
Waikapu
4616
Keahua
Makawao
Kailua Gulch
Haleakala Gulch
Wailua State Park
Nahiku
Launiupoko Pt.
Kaiwaloa Heiau
Olowalu Petroglyphs
MOKULELE HWY
AQUEDUCT
Pukalani
37
Kula Pipeline
Waikamoi Stream
Keanae Valley
Puaa Kaa Falls State Park
Piilanihale Heiau
Kalahu Point
Olowalu
Hekili Point
HONOAPIILANI HWY
Kealia Pond
Kolaloa Gulch
Olinda
38
Honomanu Strm.
Puohokamoa Strm.
Heleikeleaha Stream
Hononmaele
HANA AIR
Waianapanapa State Park
Mopua
Maalaea
Papawai Pt.
Maalaea Bay
Kihei
35
31
Kulanihakoi Gulch
Pulehu
Waiakoa
Puu Nianiau 6849
Hosmer Grove Campground
Koolau Gap
Silversword Loop
Hanakauhi
8907
Pohaku Palaha
8105
Kaeleku
36
Nan Ham
Kaluaihakoko
Kalama-Kamaole Beach Park
Kamaole
Kulanihakoi Gulch
Kaonoulu
Park Headquarters
378
Holua Cabin
Kalahaku Overlook
9324
Kaahumanu Birthplace
Hana
Keawakapu
KIHEI ROAD
Keokea
Kula Sanatorium
Haleakala Observatory
Red Hill
10023
HALEAKALA CRATER
HALEAKALA NATIONAL
PARK
Kapalaoa Cabin
Paliku Cabin
Kaupo Gap
Waihoi Valley
Wailua Falls
Kipahulu Valley
Waiohonu Strm.
HANA HWY
Ha
Moka
Puuiki
Haou
Muolea
Muolea Pt.
KULA HIGHWAY
Poli Poli Springs State Park
Kaupo Gap
Pahihi Gulch
AQUEDUCT
Kanekauila Heiau
Loaloa Heiau
Koali
Wailua Cove
Seven Sacred Pools
Puhilele Point
Makena
Ulupalakua
Puu Olai 360
Puu Mahoe 2600
37
Kula Pipeline
Kalaeinakani Gulch
Nuu
Nuu Heiau
Kaupo
Manalu Bay Petroglyphs
Kailio Point
Apole Pt.
Mokulau
Kipahulu
Molokini Island 156
Kanaio
Pimoe 1766
Lualailua Hills 1961
PIILANI HWY
31
Nakaohu Point
Ahihi Bay
Nukuele Pt. (Cape Kinau)
La Perouse Bay
Keoneoio
Waiakapuhi Burial Caves
Kanaloa Pt.
Cape Hanamanioa
Kamanamana Pt.
Pohakueaea Pt.

Auau Channel

Alalakeiki Channel

Alenuihaha Channel

Kukui Point
1443
Ule Point
Kanapou Bay
Halona Pt.
KAHOOLAWE
1161
Kealaikahiki Point
531
Kamohio Bay
Kuakaiwa Pt.
Kaka Point

0   5   10
STATUTE MILES

Original map was created in 1970.

MAUI AND KAHO'OLAWE

"Maui no kā 'oi, Maui is the best," proclaim her people, proud of their serene land, upon which the sun shines with special favor since he was slowed in his course by the folk-hero for whom the island is named. Second to Hawai'i in size, Maui was formed by two volcanoes: Pu'u Kukui, sundered by eruptions and erosion into the spectacular gorges which give "The Valley Isle" its nickname; and Haleakalā, 10,023 feet high, which encloses the world's largest dormant caldera, 21 miles in circumference. This year tourists and cattle help to sustain Maui's 141,783 residents. Gourmet pineapple and a sugar plantation are reminders of these historic industries.

Only wild goats and sheep live on Kaho'olawe, which was used as a bombing target by America's armed forces since 1942 before litigation forced an end in 1990. Today the Kaho'olawe Island Reserve Commission (KIRC) oversees the island and has led a more than 10-year period of ordnance removal and restoration effort. In 2003 control of access to the island was given to the State of Hawai'i.

1

LAHAINA was an important rest-and-recreation place for whalers from 1820 to 1860.

2

LAHAINA LUNA SCHOOL, oldest American school west of the Rocky Mountains, was founded in 1831.

3

THE SUGAR CANE TRAIN lures islanders, eager to enjoy the five-mile ride aboard the state's only passenger train.

4

LA PEROUSE BAY commemorates the five-hour visit of that ill-fated commander and his expedition on May 29, 1786. Those French explorers were the first foreigners to set foot on Maui.

5

WAILUKU is the capital of Maui Country (which includes Moloka'i and Lāna'i).

6

'IAO NEEDLE Near the heart of Pu'u Kukui's shattered crater, approaching from Wailuku through narrow 'Iao Valley, rises 'Iao Needle, 2,250 feet high.

7

HĀMĀKUA DITCH Two great irrigation systems bring water from Haleakalā's rainy northern slopes to dry Pā'ia and Pu'unene. The first system, Hāmākua Ditch, 17 miles long, constructed in 1876-1877 at a cost of $80,000 by Henry P. Baldwin and Samuel T. Alexander, showed island sugar planters how science could tame nature to serve their needs.

8

HALEAKALĀ At the top of Haleakalā, House of the Sun, where Maui-of-the-Thousand-Tricks snared the impatient sun, men and instruments in "Science City" now study the sun and track the courses of machines sent from earth into space.

9

SILVERSWORD The rare silversword, *Argyroxiphium sandwicensis*, grows near Haleakalā's summit and in its crater.

10

MAKAWAO RODEO, held on or about July 4, presents island cowboys (of varied ancestry, hue, and size) in the usual Wild West events (complete with parade) in an idyllic Hawaiian setting.

Mookini Heiau · Upolu Point
Kamehameha I Birthplace · *UPOLU AIRPORT*
Kamehameha Statue
Haena · Kapaau Kohala · Niulii · Akoakoa Point
Mahukona Beach · Paokalani I.
Mahukona
K O K o h a l a M t s.
Lahikiola 3383
27
Kahua Ranch
Malae Point
Waiilikahi Falls
Pakaalana Waipio Bay
Heiau · Waipio · Kukuihaele · Kamakamaka Pt.
24 · Haina
5505 · Honokaa · Paahau
Kawaihae · Waiaka Waimea (Kamuela)
Puukohola Heiau · 19
Kawaihae Mauna Kea · Parker Ranch Hdqrs.
Bay Beach Hotel · Paauilo · Kukaiau · Ookala
1214 · *KAMUELA AIRPORT*
Hapuna Beach Park · Holoholoku 3265 · Umikoa · Laupahoehoe Pt.
Puako · Makahalau · Laupahoehoe Papaaloa
Waawaa Point · Hanaipoe · *Maulua Bay*
Petroglyphs · Nohonaohae · Ninole
Anaehoomalu Bay · Puu Hinai · Keanakolu · Honohina
Kapalaoa · Anaehoomalu · 1439 · 3249 · Hakalau
Keawaiki · Papalekoki · Wailea
Kiholo Bay · Waikii 11448 · Hopuwai · Honomu
Kiholo · Keamuku · 8773 · 12414 · Akaka Falls State Park · Pepeekeo Point
Kaupulehu · Lake Waiau · Mauna Kea Observatory · Pepeekeo
Kawili Pt. · Kilohana Girl · Mauna Kea · Onomea
Makalawena · Puuanahulu · Scout Camp 7042 · 13796 · Paihaaloa · Onomea Bay
Mahaiula · Puu Waawaa Ranch · Puu Waawaa · Pua Akala · Papaikou
Keahole Pt. · Huehue Ranch · 3249 · Puu Ka Pele 5766 · Paukaa
Wawaloli · 6141 · Pohakuloa Camp · Laumaia · 19 · Hilo Bay
Beach · Kalaoa · 5986 · Rainbow Falls · Keaukaha
Petroglyphs · Palani · 8271 · Humuula · 7091 · Boiling Pots · Hilo · *GENERAL LYMAN FIELD*
Honokohau · Junction · Hualalai · Saddle · Puu Oo Ranch · Kaumana Caves · Papai
Kaiwi Point · *KONA AIRPORT* · Pohakuloa · Humuula · Kaumana · Orchid Gardens · Wahine Maka Nui
Kailua Bay · Kailua · 6064 · Ahu a Umi Heiau · 20 · Liliuokalani Gardens · Haena
Kauakaiakaola Heiau · Holualoa · Kokoolau · 3454 · Keaau Ranch · Kaloli Point
Disappearing · 8049 · 7049 · (Olaa) Keaau
Sands Beach · Kahaluu · Keauhou Holua Slide · 130 · Kurtistown · Makuu
Keauhou · 5200 · Solomons · Kukui · Honolulu Landing
Keauhou Bay · Water Hole · Puu Makaala
Kainaliu · 9307 · Rest · Kulani Prison · 3707 · Lehua · Mountain View · Cape
Captain Cook · Weather Station · House · 11 · Kumu
Captain Cook Monument · 8835 · 13018 · HAWAII VOLCANOES · Glenwood · Pahoa · Kapoho
Kealakekua · Pauahi · Mauna Loa · Rest House · Lava Tree State Park
Hikiau Heiau · 5422 · 13680 · Volcano House · 1071 · 132
Kealakekua Bay · Keei · Keanapaakai · Mokuaweoweo Crater · Volcano Observatory · Park Headquarters · Pohoiki
Honaunau · 12805 · Park Headquarters · 1711 · Mahinaaka
CITY OF REFUGE · Keokea · Pohaku Hanalei · Volcano · McKenzie Sta
NAT. HIST. PARK · Kilauea Crater · Kilauea Iki Crater · 137 · Opihikao
Kealia · Komakawai · Halemaumau · Fern Jungle · Kalalua Crater
Hookena · Puu Pili · Lua Manu Crater · Kane Nui o Hamo · Kaimu
Kalahiki Beach · Puu Pohakuloa · 5113 · Pauahi Crater · Napau Crater · Queen's Bath · Black Sand Beach
6222 · Kau · Makaopuhi Crater · Kupaahu
Kauluoa Point · Desert · Aloi Crater · Kalapana
Great Lava · NATIONAL PARK · Wahaula Heiau
Kipahoehoe Bay · Fissure · Great Crack · 2633 · Hilina Pali · 1050 · Holei
Papa Bay · Wood Valley Camp · Puu Kapukapu · Pali · Kaena Point
Miloli · Ohia Mill · 6870 · Pahala · (Sacred Hill) · Kealakomo
Papa · Wright Camp · Naliikakani Pt. · Keauhou Landing · Apua Point
Hoopuloa · Hilea · Kuee
Hanamalo Point · 1633 · Punaluu · Kapaoo Point
Okoe Bay · Manuka State Park · Ninole
Kamoi Point · 2992 · Honuapo · *Kawa Bay*
Manuka Bay · Waiohinu · Honuapo Bay
Kahuku Ranch · Naalehu
Kauna Point · Kolukahi · *Waikapuna Bay*
Pohue Bay · Petroglyphs · Kaalualu · *Kaalualu Bay*
Heiau o Molilele
Waiahukini · Pacific Missile Range Facility · Mahana Bay
Heiau o Kalalea · Ka Lae (South Cape)

| 0 | 5 | 10 | 15 | 20 |
STATUTE MILES

Original map was created in 1970.

HAWAI'I

"The Big Island," with 4,028 square miles, has been formed by lava flows issuing from five volcanic rift-zones. The oldest, in Kohala, is inactive; Hualalai, which last erupted in 1801, and Mauna Kea probably are dormant; Mauna Loa and Kīlauea, still very much awake, are the most active volcanoes on earth. For this reason, the red 'ōhi'a lehua blossom, sacred to the fire goddess Pele, is the island's official flower.

Today more than 170,000 people live on Hawai'i. Its economy was once based upon five sugar plantations and numerous cattle ranches. These have given way to diversified agriculture. Traditional businesses include vegetable farms and nurseries for orchids; tropical flowers and foliage; orchards for coffee, macadamia nuts, and fruits; lumbering; and services for tourists.

1

KALĀHIKIOLA CHURCH In peaceful Kohala, look for unspoiled Pololū Valley and unexpected evidence of New England at Kalāhikiola Church, built in 1855.

2

MAUNA KEA Upon Mauna Kea's highest peaks, above clouds and dust, astronomers study the stars through 12 telescopes at this internationally known observatory.

3

HULIHE'E PALACE In Kailua are Hulihe'e Palace, constructed for High Chief Kuakini in 1837-1838, and Moku'aikaua Church, begun in 1836.

4

PARKER RANCH, more than 300,000 acres in extent, is about three-fourths the size of O'ahu.

5

KEALAKEKUA BAY Captain James Cook, Western discoverer of the Hawaiian Islands, and four of his marines were killed in a fight at Kealakekua Bay on February 14, 1779.

6

THE CITY OF REFUGE at Hōnaunau, handsomely restored by the U.S. National Park Service in 1967-1969, shows how effectively the ancient Hawaiians used their island's resources of stone and wood.

7

KAIMŪ BEACH Lava rather than coral forms the black sand of Kaimū Beach near Kalapana.

8

MAUNA KEA BEACH HOTEL Near Kawaihae, elegant Mauna Kea Beach Hotel stands in contrast to Kamehameha's war temple of Pu'u Kohola, largest *heiau* in the islands.

9

HAWAI'I VOLCANOES NATIONAL PARK, created by Congress in 1916, is the abode of the fire goddess Pele. The park includes Moku'āweoweo, Mauna Loa's summit caldera, as well as the chain of craters which identifies the Kīlauea rift zone.

10

HILO is Hawai'i County's capital, major port, and site of the University of Hawai'i's second campus.

11

WAIPI'O VALLEY, once the home of Kohala's warring chiefs and their subjects, is quieter now, peopled by taro farmers.

TREES

Hawai'i's flora is as cosmopolitan as are her people: somewhere in the islands, between seashore and mountain tops, a place has been found for adopted plants imported from many alien parts of the world. This diversity is most evident in the trees and flowering shrubs: cryptomerias from Japan grow among eucalypts from Australia, and frangipani from Central America bloom at the feet of towering Norfolk Island pines.

Aboriginal Hawaiians started the transformation of these new-found islands when they brought the ancestral coconuts, *kukui*, breadfruits, mountain apples, and bananas, as well as many other food plants and medicinal herbs, from central Polynesia. In 1792 Captain George Vancouver and Dr. Archibald Menzies, his surgeon-naturalist, inaugurated the age of modern introductions when they presented Kona's chiefs with several hundred young orange plants grown from seeds obtained at the Cape of Good Hope. During the nineteenth century, sea captains and residents brought in dozens of new species of trees. Since 1900 government agencies and the Hawaiian Sugar Planters' Association Experiment Station have been responsible for establishing trees suitable as windbreaks or in forestation projects, and commercial nurseries have specialized in flowering ornamentals.

POINCIANA, flamboyant, *Delonix regia*; from Madagascar. Relatively small trees, with buttressing roots, twisted trunk, gnarled, irregular branches. In spring, masses of scarlet flowers touched with orange and gold burst out from every branch tip, seeming to set the tree ablaze.

MĀMANE, *Sophora chrysophylla*; endemic. Leguminous shrubs to trees; prefer high elevations; clusters of pale yellow flowers at branch tips and leaf axils; winged pods bear 4 to 8 oval yellow seeds. Hawaiians used the exceedingly hard wood for sled-runners, digging sticks, and posts.

COCONUT PALM, *Cocos nucifera*; from Indo-Pacific region, "the best known palm in the world." Imported by colonizing Hawaiians as one of their essential plants, it provided food, drink, shelter, wood, cordage, ornaments, medicine, and cosmetics.

KIAWE, mesquite, *Prosopis pallida*; from Peru. Shrubs to large trees. Feathery mimosa-like leaves: long, sharp thorns on young branches; pale yellow florets in cylindrical spikes, long, stiff yellow pods. It enriches soil; yields nectar for honey, beans for cattle fodder, wood for charcoal.

KUKUI, candlenut, *Aleurites moluccana*; from southern Asia. Erect, tall trees; large, yellow-green to green maplelike leaves; clusters of small white flowers; fleshy green fruits enclosing one or two black nuts. Hawaiians burned nutmeats (or their oil) for light, made ornaments of the polished shells.

MONKEYPOD, *Samanea saman*; from Central America. Large spreading trees, forming great domes of dark green leaves; feathery pink puffs of flowers appear in spring, followed by long, dark, wrinkled pods. Bowls, trays, furniture are made from beautifully grained wood.

GOLDEN SHOWER, Indian laburnum, *Cassia fistula*; from India. Tall trees, with dark green compound leaves composed of 4 to 8 pairs of broad, pointed leaflets; large, drooping clusters of brilliant yellow flowers; straight, dark brown, cylindrical seed pods 1 to 2 feet long.

TRAVELERS' TREE, *Ravenala madagascarensis*; from Madagascar. This strange plant resembles flattened banana leaves grafted upon a palm stump, bearing gigantic white birds-of-paradise for flowers. Rainwater collected at the base of each leaf can be tapped by thirsty travelers.

INDIAN BANYAN, *Ficus benghalensis*; from India. Enormous spreading trees, with thick central trunks, huge arching branches supported by stiltlike secondary trunks formed by aerial rootlets. Canopy of dark green ovate leaves with pairs of small, round, cherry-red fruits.

NATIVE BIRDS

Only a few kinds of land birds accidentally found their way across the more than 2,000 miles of ocean that separate the Hawaiian Islands from North America and Asia. About 15 ancestral species from 11 families of birds did reach the islands in the distant past. In the absence of competition and predators, these ancestors evolved to form about 70 different kinds of ducks and a hawk, one entire family is found only in the Hawaiian Islands. This is the Hawaiian honeycreeper family (Drepanididae). The honeycreepers illustrate the process of organic evolution on isolated oceanic islands to a finer degree than any other bird family in the world. Unfortunately, about 40 percent of these unique Hawaiian birds already are extinct. Another third are rare and endangered. This is a tragic situation because when a species of plants or animal becomes extinct, it is lost forever.

'APAPANE *right*

The 'Apapane, *Himatione sanguinea*, is the most common of the surviving species of honeycreepers, and is found on all the main Hawaiian Islands. Gregarious during much of the year and vociferous in the nesting season, the 'apapane frequents the tops of forest trees. When it feeds on the bright red flowers of the 'ōhi'a lehua, the 'apapane may be hard to see, even though its body feathers are deep crimson.

'I'IWI *far right*

Few birds are as striking as the brilliant orange-red 'I'iwi, *Vestiaria coccinea*, with its black wings and tail and long, curved, salmon-colored bill. The birds feed on insects and a variety of flowers, including the endemic lobelia. Abundant on all main islands in the 1890s, now the 'i'iwi is common only on Kaua'i, Maui, and Hawai'i.

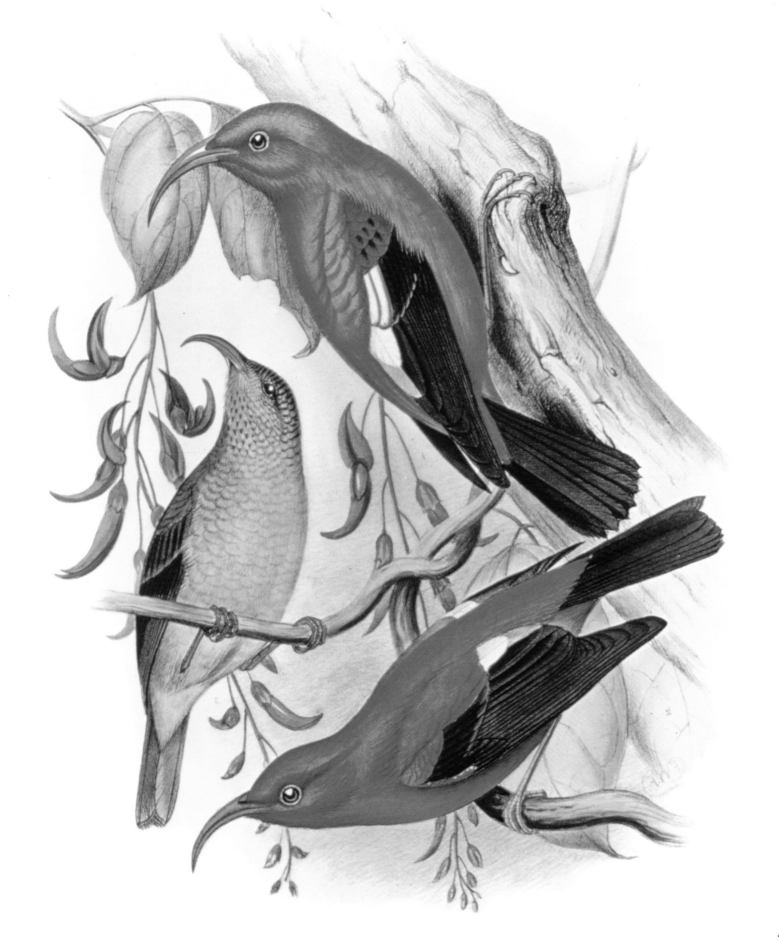

'ELEPAIO *below left*

The *'Elepaio, Chasiempis sandwichensis*, is an Old World flycatcher that inhabits the forests of Kaua'i, O'ahu, and Hawai'i. Less than six inches in total length, the *'elepaio* is an inquisitive bird, often hopping from branch to branch close to a person standing still in the forest. Perhaps because of one of its primary songs, "'e-le-pa-i-o," this bird was important in Hawaiian folklore.

'IO *right*

The *'Io*, or Hawaiian Hawk, *Buteo solitarius*, is one of the endangered species. It is a diurnal bird of prey that lives primarily on mice, rats, spiders, and insects. The females, about 18 inches in length, are larger than the males. These broad-winged, soaring birds are found only on the island of Hawai'i.

MAMO *below right*

The Black Mamo, or 'O'o-nuku-mū, *Drepanis funerea*, a honeycreeper, subsisted almost entirely on nectar, and was especially partial to the tubular flowers of several species of lobelia. The birds often fed only a foot or so from the ground. As a bird inserted its bill deeply into a flower, the sticky, whitish pollen adhered to the feathers on the top of the bird's head, and thus was carried to other flowers. The birds usually were tame, not infrequently following a person through the forest, and responding to imitations of their calls. The Black Mamo was discovered on Moloka'i by R.C. L. Perkins in 1893. The birds were not common, and the last specimens were collected about 1907. No one has seen a *mamo* since those times.

'O'O *far right*

Once termed the "prince, or king, of Hawaiian plumage-birds," the Hawai'i 'O'o, *Moho nobilis*, a honeyeater, was first collected during the visit of Captain Cook's expedition in 1779. The birds were more than a foot in length, and their yellow feathers were highly valued by Hawaiians for making feather capes and headdresses. It has been estimated that yellow feathers from nearly 80,000 'o'o and *mamo*, *Drepanis pacifica*, were used to make the splendid feather cloak of Kamehameha the Great. Although considered a common bird in the early 1890s, the last of the magnificent 'o'o apparently were killed soon after the turn of the century. Only the Kaua'i 'O'o, which has fewer yellow feathers than any of the other species, was found in Alaka'i Marsh but not seen since 1982 after Hurricane 'Iwa.

Illustrations from Walter Rothschild. 1893-1900.
"The Avifauna of Laysan and the Hawaiian
Possessions," and S.B. Wilson and A.H. Evans.
1890-1899. "Aves Hawaiienses."

NATIVE PLANTS

The native flora, once upon a time, consisted of about 1800 species, 96 percent of which grew nowhere else in the world. Many of these endemic plants have been exterminated or overwhelmed by people, animals, microbes, or plants imported from foreign lands.

If they survive, native plants grow now in mountain retreats or in remote valleys untouched by progress. Notable among these products of evolutionary isolation, and made only in Hawai'i, are the graceful koa, whose expanded, flat, crescent leaf-stem soon replaces the leaflets typical of acacias; the silversword, adapted to the alpine heights of Maui and Hawai'i; the even rarer greensword of Haleakalā; handsome tree lobelia, whose flowers are curved to the shape of the beaks of the endemic birds, which sipped their nectar. Many are beautiful, as these watercolors attest. They were painted in the 1880s by Mrs. Francis Sinclair, Jr., of Makaweli, Kaua'i.

Hawai'i's lush flora, like its people and its animals, is borrowed from almost everywhere else: 99 percent of the plants seen today upon our shores and plains are not native to Hawai'i. Since 1778 almost 2,000 kinds of new plants have been introduced either intentionally or accidentally. Before 1850 most of those were food plants or weeds. Since that time, ornamentals and forest trees have been favored. Many importations, such as Java plum, algarroba, lantana, Christmas berry, ironwood, silver oak, brassaia, tibouchina, bamboos, three kinds of guavas, and other grasses, even the graceful palms and fragrant gingers, have escaped from cultivation, to take conspicuous places in the Hawaiian landscape.

Before the foreigners arrived, with all their

left to right
'IE'IE, climbing screwpine, *Freycinetia arborea*
'ŌHI'A LEHUA, *Metrosideros collina*
subsp. *polymorpha*
'UKI'UKI, *Dianella ensifolia*

Illustrations from Mrs. Francis Sinclair, Jr. 1885.
"Indigenous Flowers of the Hawaiian Islands."

exotic plants, animals, textiles, tools, and machines, Hawaiians relied heavily upon the plants, which Nature or their ancestors had established in the islands. Because they had no metals, no clay, no tools other than those they fashioned from stones, pieces of wood, or splinters of shell and bone, Hawaiians had learned to use plant materials in many ingenious ways. From one part or another of those plants they obtained shelter, clothing, tools, utensils, ornaments, dyes, light, medicines, as well as motifs in art and talismans to protect them from the magic of sorcerers or the wrath of the gods.

They had given names to herbs, shrubs, and trees and classified them according to resemblances, real or fancied, to other familiar things. They cultivated fields or groves of edible plants, such as taro, sweet potato, breadfruit, banana and coconut, and gathered food from others such as mountain apples and *kukui* nuts, wherever they grew. Plantations of the paper mulberry, or *wauke*, provided the bark from which women made *kapa*. *'Olana* and *hau* gave the fibers from which men spun twine for fishnets and lashings, and coconut husks the coarse material from which they made sennit.

Each of the seven kinds of indigenous plants illustrated here by Mrs. Sinclair's watercolors yielded dyes, medicines, and either wood or thatch for shelters. The fruits of mountain apple, raspberry, and *noni* were edible, as were the aerial and underground tubers of the yam.

left to right (top)
NONI, *Morinda citrifolia*
UHI, yam, *Dioscorea alata*

left to right (bottom)
'AKALA, raspberry, *Rubus hawaiiensis*
'ŌHI'A 'AI, mountain apple, *Eugenia malaccensis*

FISHES

The ancestors of most marine plants and animals now found in Hawai'i came from the warm, fecund Indo-Pacific seas. Although North America is closer, its coastal waters have contributed little to Hawai'i's marine flora and fauna. Ocean currents and temperatures, the major factors affecting distribution of water-borne organisms, favored migrants from Indonesia or southeast Asia and blocked those from America. Ultimately, many of the immigrants, forced to adapt to new environments as they wandered and after they reached this mid-Pacific habitat, evolved into the species which biologists consider to be indigenous to Hawai'i. The numbers and kinds of reef and shore creatures differ with place, season, and depth. O'ahu's shores retain a surprising assortment of both plants and animals, but less frequented beaches on neighbor islands are more rewarding. The ecology of a Hawaiian reef is revealed most clearly in the exhibit at Sea Life Park.

left to right (top row)
Scarus dubius
Antigonia steindachneri
Chaetodon trifasciatus

left to right (middle row)
LAU'Ī-PALA, *Zebrasoma flavescens*
HUMUHUMU-'ELE'ELE, *Melichthys buniva*
LAU-WILIWILI-NUKUNUKU-'OI'OI, *Forcipiger longirostris*

left to right (bottom row)
PĀKU'IKU'I, *Acanthurus achilles*
PO'O PA'A, *Cirrhitus alternatus*
NOHU, *Scorpaenopsis cacopsis*

Illustrations from David Starr Jordan and Barton W. Evermann, 1905.
"The Aquatic Resources of the Hawaiian Islands."

The ocean has always been the primary source of edible fish for Hawaiians because the islands lack extensive rivers and lakes. Ichthyologists have identified about 600 species more or less indigenous to Hawaiian waters, ranging in size from huge sharks to inconspicuous things smaller than the *humu* in *humuhumunukunukuapua'a*. New discoveries are made each year as methods for collecting specimens in deeper waters are improved. Biologists in research submarines, while exploring the submerged slopes off western O'ahu, have seen great numbers of marine creatures, both known and new to science, living in that fertile zone.

The state has established several undersea parks, with marked trails, for skin-divers and scuba-divers who prefer to look at fish rather than catch them. The deeper waters off the leeward coasts present sportfishermen with record-breaking marlin, broadbill, sailfish, *mahimahi*, and tuna. Others enjoy displays at Waikīkī Aquarium and Sea Life Park.

left to right (top row)
HUMUHUMU-NUKUNUKU-A-PUA'A,
    Rhinecanthus aculeatus
MĀLOLO, *Parexocoetus brachypterus*
Chaetodon miliaris

left to right (middle row)
KIKIKAPU, *Holocanthus arcuatus*
PĀ'Ū'Ū, *Myripristis chryseres*
KIHIKIHI, *Zanclus canescens*

left to right (bottom row)
Holotrachys lima
KALA, *Naso unicornis*
'Ō'ILI 'UWI'UWI, *Pervagor spilosoma*

58

59

FRUITS AND VEGETABLES

The diet of aboriginal Hawaiians was adequate but dull. For fruits they had only mountain apples in their short season, sugarcane, and bananas; for vegetables, only taro, breadfruit, sweet potatoes, yams, coconuts, *kukui* nuts, ti roots, some kinds of seaweeds and ferns. Foreigners realized from the beginning that, for everyone's sake, the islands' stock of food plants must be diversified. Captain Cook himself left seeds of pumpkins, melons, and onions at Ni'ihau in 1778. By 1800 Hawaiian farmers had learned from Europeans how to "rear to perfection" watermelons, muskmelons, strawberries, oranges, and many common vegetables. Indefatigable Don Marin introduced other vegetables and a variety of fruits now widespread: guavas, pineapples, limes, lemons, prickly pears, and mangoes.

Settlers from Asia imported seeds or stocks of plants needed in preparing their favorite foods, or just to provide a taste of home: fruits like persimmon, lychee, Satsuma orange, dragon's eye, and pommelo; and such vegetables as *daikon, won bok, gobo, dasheen*, soybean, rice, bitter melon, and eggplant. Today an appetizing blend of foods and recipes from East and West is served in homes and restaurants.

PINEAPPLES Don Marin planted the first pineapples in 1813. The Smooth Cayenne variety, formerly the major crop for island plantations, was introduced in 1885. Maui Gold is today's gourmet pineapple.

LIMES and lemons of many varieties have been introduced, mostly from Asia, since Don Marin planted the first lime seedling in his vineyard in Honolulu.

BREADFRUIT, originally from Malaysia, wa brought to Pacific islands by migrating Polynesian. Well-ripened breadfruit, baked or steamed, is a trea for gourmets.

GUAVA Don Marin introduced the guava, native to tropical America, about 1825. Its sour fruits yield superlative juice, jams, and jellies.

MANGO In 1824 Captain John Meek Honolulu brought Don Marin some "common mango seedlings from Manila.

LYCHEE The first lychee seedling from China was planted in Hawai'i in 1873. Most delicious when fresh, the grape-like fruits can be preserved by freezing or drying.

YAMS True yams, *Dioscorea alata*, are rarely seen anymore, although Captain Cook bought them in quantities at Kaua'i and Ni'ihau. Most "yams" sold in markets today are varieties of sweet potatoes.

SUGARCANE The first Hawaiians brought sugarcane with them from the central Pacific. Island plantations grow inter-specific hybrids.

PAPAYA, native to tropical America, provides islanders' favorite breakfast fruit, and the enzyme papain, used in biological research and as a meat tenderizer.

BANANAS "The Fruit of Paradise," as Europeans called bananas, originated in India. Hawaiians grew about 50 varieties, few of which survived.

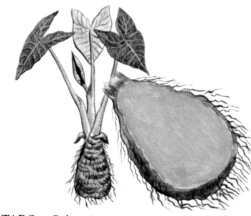

TARO is Polynesians' most important starchfood. The cooked corms, pounded into a smooth paste and mixed with water, make *poi*. The tender leaves, called *lū'au*, are better than spinach.

PASSION FRUIT Although many species of passion fruit grow wild in Hawai'i, only the yellow *liliko'i* is cultivated commercially. The complex flowers, whose parts symbolize the passion of Christ, give these plants their common name.

CHINESE CABBAGE, or *won bok*, prime ingredient in *kim chee*, was one of the first vegetables introduced from Asia.

61

HOLIDAYS AND CELEBRATIONS

1

MAKAHIKI DAY is observed by school children and cultural practicners in November. Ancient Hawai'i's Makahiki season was from October through January, when people met at friendly sports contests rather than upon a field of battle.

2

KAMEHAMEHA DAY If Hawai'i were still a monarchy, June 11 would be our most important national holiday. Started almost a hundred years ago to honor Kamehameha I, it recalls now, in parades, pageants, *lū'au*, *hula*, and a climactic glittering grand ball, the glamour and the beauty of the lost Kingdom of Hawai'i.

3

CHRISTMAS Everyone, regardless of race or creed, is caught up in the great feast of Christmas. According to his whim, Santa Claus arrives by canoe, surfboard, jet plane, or helicopter but never in a sled drawn by eight reindeer.

4

WESAK About the time Christians celebrate Easter, many Asians celebrate the birthday of Buddha with Wesak or, as it is called in Japanese, Hanamatsuri, the Flower Festival.

5

CHINESE NEW YEAR (which, depending upon the moon, comes a month or so after that of the Western calendar) is greeted with fireworks, feasting, lion dancers, flowering narcissus plants, and delectable confections.

6

BOYS' DAY, for Japanese families, is May 5. Those heroic fish, flying like kites from a pole above a boy's home and symbolic Japan's carp, are made of oiled paper or cloth, or of plastic. They are gifts from friends, urging him to heed this example of strong persevering carp. Girls have their "Doll Day" on March 3.

7

SAMOAN FLAG DAY is August 15, when the Samoan community commemorates America's annexation of eastern Samoa in 1900 with feasting, cultural exhibits, singing, and dancing.

8

BABY LŪ'AU A happy custom, borrowed from party-loving Hawaiians, is the baby *lū'au*, presented in celebration of a child's first birthday.

9

MEMORIAL DAY The dead of all races and religions are honored on America's Memorial Day, May 30. Especially poignant are the ceremonies and the flowers for those who are buried in the National Memorial Cemetery of the Pacific, within Punchbowl's green, quiet crater.

10

BON ODORI Throughout the summer, especially in August, Japanese Buddhists remember the spirits of relatives who have died during the past year with somber rituals at temples and shrines, and with the happy dances of Bon Odori. At these gatherings, which, with their food booths and resounding orchestras that resemble village fairs, relatives and spectators alike can join in the posturing dances.

11

LEI DAY Since 1928 "May Day Is Lei Day in Hawai'i." This most endemic of Hawai'i's festivals is popular throughout the islands. Residents in smaller communities find time to make *lei*, and their children in school present ceremonial pageants to entertain their Lei Queen and her court.

12

FLORES DE MAYO is a Filipino festival imported from the home country. Youths and maidens in Philippine costumes honor the Blessed Virgin Mary, Christian saints, and universal virtues with candle-lit processions, flowers, songs, and dances.

1

5

3

4

7

8

0

11

12

A SAMPLING OF LOCAL EXPRESSIONS

Among themselves, islanders communicate in a language loaded with words and phrases borrowed from their several parent cultures. Children learn these polyglot vocabularies as naturally as they acquire relatives and friends, or develop a taste for cokes, *sushi*, *see mui*, and TV. But *haole* who want to use these terms should select them with caution and pronounce them with care. Hawaiian words especially, rich in double- and triple- meanings or ribald improprieties, can be embarrasing traps for the uninstructed. Genuine pidgin-English, seldom spoken anymore, has been replaced by a debased dialect that employs English words sloppily pronounced, a syntax reduced to essentials, staccato speed, and swooping rhythms.

HAWAI'I NEI: All the islands in the group, to distinguish them from the Big Island of Hawai'i alone.

PĀ'Ū: A skirt, which may be simple and short, or as voluminous as the colorful drapery worn by a pā'ū rider in the Kamehameha Day parade.

LEI HULU: *Lei* made of feathers, rare and costly even in olden times, were worn only by female chiefs of great rank.

KAPŪ: The Hawaiian form of that well-known word, taboo. Used as a noun, it means a rule or prohibition, or something forbidden; used as a verb (most often on signs) it means KEEP OUT.

SEE MUI: Chinese plums, soaked in brine, then dried. Undoubtedly the saltiest preserve known to man. A great selection of preserved fruits—crackseed, mango seed, sweet-sour seed, wet seed, dry seed, and a host of others—are imported from Hong Kong and Taiwan.

HAOLE: The term originates from *ha*, meaning breath, and *'ole*, which means without — "without breath." Ancient Hawaiians called the first white men *haole* because they did not know how to perform the Hawaiian greeting of touching nose-to-nose and inhaling, essentially sharing each other's breath. *Ha* is important in the Hawaiian culture because it represents life. Today the term is usually used to define people not from Hawai'i.

ZORI: Japanese flat sandals or slippers, formerly made of woven rice straw, now mass-produced in rubber. **GETA:** Japanese wooden clogs, with cross-pieces of wood 1 to 4 inches high. **TABI:** the Japanese sock, resembling a mitten more than a stocking.

'A'Ā: Rough, fragmented lava; as opposed to *pahoehoe*: smooth, unbroken lava. The terms have been adopted by geologists throughout the world.

SASHIMI: Japan's major contribution to Hawai'i's *pūpū* set: very thin slices of raw fish, served on a snow-white nest of crisp, cool *daikon*.

'OKOLE MALUNA: A literal (but vulgar) translation into Hawaiian of the drinkers' salute, "Bottoms up."

ALOHA: Hello, goodbye, love, affection, regard and how-do-you-do?

'ULĪ'ULĪ (and watch your pronunciation!): Gour rattles, topped with dyed feathers, which hul dancers shake so expertly.

HUKILAU: If you're fortunate enough to be goin to a *hukilau*, you'll be helping a lot of other folk t pull (*huki*) a dragnet hung with leaves (*lau*) to shor By custom the owner of the seine shares the catc with his helpers.

PAU: Done, finished, ended. The one absolutel necessary Hawaiian word in every home.

"SUCK 'EM UP": Usually pronounced "Soc 'um op," and generally (but not always) referring t alcoholic beverages; this can be a toast, an expletive an invitation, or a cheering exhortation, dependin upon speaker and circumstances.

KAUKAU: Slang for food of any kind. When it's delicious, the *kaukau* is *'ono.*

PŪPŪ: The Hawaiian word for shells from sea or land; also used for hors d'oeuvres and cocktail-party snacks.

MU'UMU'U: Deformed or shapeless, cut-off, maimed; a loose-fitting dress similar to the Mother Hubbard in nursery rhymes.

HOLOKŪ: A fitted dress, with a yoke and sometimes a train, an elegant style from the Hawaiian monarchy period.

LŪ'AU: A native Hawaiian feast, so called because *lū'au,* taro leaves, usually cooked with coconut cream and pork or chicken, are a featured dish.

LAULAU: A package of food, wrapped in ti leaves, containing morsels of pork or beef and fish, enclosed in taro, or *kalo,* leaves.

MABUHAY: Hello, or greetings, in Tagalog, a Filipino dialect.

DA KINE: A corruption of "that kind," a useful pidgin generalization that often confuses newcomers.

SUSHI: Cold rice with a core of pickled vegetables and/or fish; called *inarizushi* when stuffed into a cone of golden soybean curd (tofu), *makizushi* when rolled in cylinders enclosed in casings of dried black seaweed.

KAMA'ĀINA: Literally, "a child of the land," born and raised in Hawai'i. A newcomer, or a guest, is a *malihini.*

MENEHUNE: The first people to settle in these islands, traditionally described as smaller and darker than later settlers from Polynesia.

MAUKA: Toward the mountains. **MAKAI:** Toward the sea. When giving directions, *kama'āina* refer to landmarks rather than to points of the compass. For example, in Honolulu, to reach 'Iolani Palace from Aloha Tower, "you go *mauka* four blocks, then *makai* three blocks."

"HAWAIIAN TIME": "A little bit late," anywhere from 5 minutes to 5 hours after the appointed time.

PUA: A *pua* is a flower. A *pua'a* is a pig. A *lū'au* presents the nicest way for the two to meet.

IMU: The Polynesian earth-oven, in which foods are cooked with heat released from hot rocks.

PALI: A cliff or precipice. "The Pali" is the one at Nu'uanu, O'ahu.

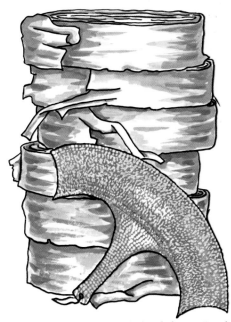

LAUHALA: The leaf of the *hala* or Pandanus tree. From these leaves, cleaned, stripped of their sawtooth edges, and stored in rolls, Polynesian plait mats, purses, fans, coasters, hats, and other articles.

SHIBUI: The Japanese word for elegant simplicity. *Shibai* is their sneer for the false, the phony, the sham.

FACT AND FICTION

Much of the fun of living in Hawai'i comes from enjoying the inventions of imaginations—that ecumenical assortment of myths, legends, superstitions, illusions, traditions, rumors, gossip, and fabrications, encrusted upon a few more or less discernible facts, around which we build our conversation and our attitudes.

We may pretend to scoff at those stories about Pele hitchhiking along the Big Island's highways, but not one of us dares to ignore a little old Tūtū, or grandma, who's out thumbing a ride. We thrill to tales about the Marchers of the Night, to accounts of houses, cemeteries, or whole forests haunted by malevolent kahuna 'anā'anā, Japanese fox spirits, Chinese devils, or pallid English ghosts. We make the prescribed offerings to resident gods when we enter their silent temples. We know that Pele lives when she holds court in her fiery palace at Kīlauea, we approach in awe, offering chants in praise of her tribute in 'ohelo berries, maile lei, but bottles of alcohol, an outdated tourist custom, are not encouraged.

And, despite all evidence to the contrary, we cherish the most persistent myth of all: the belief that always, since first men found them, these islands have been green and lovely, undespoiled and unspoilable, inhabited by people whose hearts are blessed, whose voices are lifted in song.

'UKULELE: Most people think that Hawaiians invented the 'ukulele. Actually it is a local variant of the Portuguese braguinha, introduced by contract laborers in the 1880s. Musical Hawaiians happily took it up, as earlier they had adopted the Spanish guitar.

CHINESE FIRECRACKERS: Scare devils and evil spirits from feasts, weddings, and funerals.

ALOE BARBADENSIS: Leaf sap (mispronounced "ah loy" by folk who think the name is Hawaiian) used in treating burns, cuts, and skin infections.

GRASS SKIRT: Hula dancers adopted the grass skirt from Micronesian immigrants in the 1880s. Skirts made of ti leaves, cellophane, or plastic are later variations.

NU'UANU PALI: At the battle of Nu'uanu in 1795, Kamehameha's armies won by forcing hundreds of O'ahu's defenders over the Pali. Warriors jumped or fell into the abyss, preferring honorable death to being captured and sacrificed. Their bones were found when the Pali Highway was built in the late 1950s.

LAE 'AHI: The Hawaiians' name for Diamond Head, because Hi'iaka, Pele's younger sister, compared it with the brow (lae) of the 'ahi, the yellow-fin tuna. The haole name dates from 1825, when British sailors thought that "Pele's tears" formed in the mountain's lava were diamonds.

SACRED FALLS VALLEY: A narrow cleft in the Ko'olau Range near Hau'ula on O'ahu is a fine example of stream-erosion. According to legend, however, it was scored into the mountain by cloven hoofs of Kamapua'a, the mischievous pig god, when he leaped over the steep ridge to escape hunters he had angered. Kamapua'a still frequents the place, and people who enter his abode placate him with offerings of leaves each time they cross the valley's little stream, if they don't want him to hurl rocks upon them from the high cliffs above.

KIM CHEE: A Korean dish of a mouth-watering, belly-warming combination of salted, pickled Chinese cabbage and other vegetables, suffused with garlic and braced with chili peppers.

'ŌHI'A LEHUA: "Plucking an 'ōhi'a lehua blossom will bring rain," said the people of old. Usually the prophecy is fulfilled because 'ōhi'a lehua trees grow best in rain country.

SUGGESTED READING

ABRAMSON, JOAN. 1976. *Photographers of Old Hawaii*. Honolulu: Island Heritage Limited.

APPLE, RUSS and PEG. 1977. *Tales of Old Hawaii*. Honolulu: Island Heritage Limited.

BALCOMB, KENNETH. (Date?). *The Whales of Hawaii*. Honolulu: Island Heritage.

BARROW, TERENCE. 1976. *Captain Cook in Hawaii*. Honolulu: Island Heritage Limited.

BERGER, ANDREW J. 1977. *The Exotic Birds of Hawaii*. Honolulu: Island Heritage Limited.

CAHILL, EMMETT. (Date?). *The Life and Times of John Young*. Honolulu: Island Heritage.

DAWS, A. GAVAN. 1968. *Shoal of Time*. New York: Macmillan.

DAY, A. GROVE, and CARL STROVEN. 1959. *A Hawaiian Reader*. New York: Appleton-Century-Crofts, Inc.

FEHER, JOSEPH. 1969. *Hawaii: A Pictorial History*. Honolulu: Bishop Museum Press.

FUCHS, LAWRENCE H. 1961. *Hawaii Pono: A Social History*. New York: Harcourt, Brace and World.

GOODMAN, ROBERT B., A.G. DAWS, and E. SHEEHAN. 1970. *The Hawaiians*. Honolulu: Island Heritage Limited.

GOSLINE, W.A., and VERNON BROCK. 1965. *Handbook of Hawaiian Fishes*. Honolulu: University of Hawaii Press.

HAWAII AUDUBON SOCIETY. 1967. *Hawaii's Birds*. Honolulu: Published by the Audubon Society.

I'I, JOHN PAPA. 1959. *Fragments of Hawaiian History*. Honolulu: Bishop Museum Press.

INOUYE, DANIEL K., with LAWRENCE ELLIOTT. 1967. *Journey to Washington*. Englewood Cliffs, N.J.: Prentice-Hall, Inc.

KAMAKAU, SAMUEL M. 1964. *Ka Po'e Kahiko: The People of Old*. Honolulu: Bishop Museum Press.

KANAHELE, GEORGE. 1993. *Kū Kaualea, Stand Tall: A Search for Hawaiian Values*. Honolulu: University of Hawaii Press.

KANE, HERB KAWAINUI. 1976. *Voyage: The Discovery of Hawaii*. Honolulu: Island Heritage Limited.

KRAUSS, BOB. 1990. *Our Hawai'i: The Best of Bob Krauss. A Collection of the Author's Best Stories Written for the Honolulu Advertiser*. 'Aiea: Island Heritage Publishers.

KORN, ALFONS. 1958. *The Victorian Visitors*. Honolulu: University of Hawaii Press.

KUYKENDALL, RALPH S. 1938, 1953, 1967. *The Hawaiian Kingdom*. Vol. I, 1778-1854, Foundations and Transformation. Vol. II, 1854-1874, Twenty Critical Years. Vol. III, 1874-1893, The Kalakaua Dynasty. Honolulu: University of Hawaii Press.

LOOMIS, ALBERTINE. 1951, 1966. *Grapes of Canaan*. Honolulu: Hawaiian Mission Children's Society.

MACDONALD, GORDON A., and AGATIN ABBOTT. 1970. *Volcanoes in the Sea*. Honolulu: University of Hawaii Press.

NEAL, MARIE C. 1965. *In Gardens of Hawaii*. Honolulu: Bishop Museum Press.

PUKUI, MARY KAWENA, and SAMUEL H. ELBERT, 1966. *Place Names of Hawaii*. Honolulu: University of Hawaii Press.

ROTHSCHILD, WALTER. 1893-1900. *The Avifauna of Laysan and the Hawaiian Possessions*. London: R.H. Porter.

SCHMITT, ROBERT C. 1968. *Demographic Statistics of Hawaii, 1778-1965*. Honolulu: University of Hawaii Press.

SEIDEN, ALLAN. (Date?). *The Art of the Hula*. Honolulu: Island Heritage.

SINCLAIR, MRS. FRANCIS, JR. 1885. *Indigenous Flowers of the Hawaiian Islands*. London: Sampson Low, Marston, Searle, and Rivington.

STEARNS, HAROLD T. 1966. *Geology of the State of Hawaii*. Palo Alto, California: Pacific Books.

STONE, SCOTT C. S. 1977. *Pearl Harbor: The Way it Was*. Honolulu: Island Heritage Limited.

_____. (Date?). *Yesterdays in Hawaii: A Voyage Through Time*. Honolulu: Island Heritage.